W9-BCK-641

DISCARDED BY
WELLES-TURNER
MEMORIAL LIBRARY
GLASTONBURY, CT

THE GULF WAR

A DAY-BY-DAY CHRONICLE

THE GULF WAR

A DAY-BY-DAY CHRONICLE

DR FREDERICK STANWOOD
PATRICK ALLEN LINDSAY PEACOCK

MALLARD
PRESS

Mallard Press and its accompanying design and logo
are trademarks of BDD Promotional Book Company, Inc.

Text copyright © 1991 Reed International Books
Chronology copyright © 1990-1 BBC World Service

First published in the United States of America
in 1991 by The Mallard Press in association with Octopus International.

The Chronology used in this book was originally published as The Gulf Crisis: A
Chronology. Full copies of that text can be obtained by writing to the News and
Information Library, BBC World Service, Bush House, Aldwych, London WC2

ISBN 0-7924-5649-1

All rights reserved

Printed in Great Britain

CONTENTS

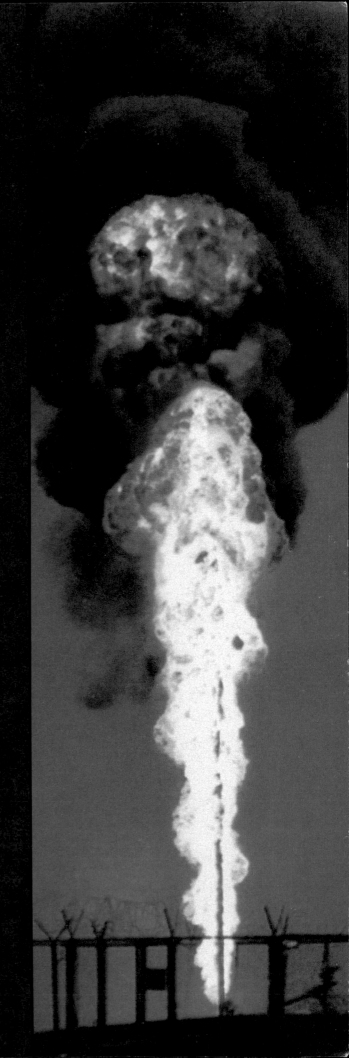

INTRODUCTION

ON the main highway to Basra, just north of Kuwait City, stands what for many people will be one of the abiding images of the Gulf War: the twisted, burnt and broken remains of hundreds of Iraqi vehicles caught in a high-technology cross-fire near the police post at Mutla. Nothing better illustrates the reality of Iraq's supposedly mighty military machine; this was a rag-tag army in disarray, attempting to escape with as much loot as it could carry. On paper, Saddam Hussein possessed the fourth largest army in the world. Intelligence estimates prior to the start of the air campaign put the total Iraqi force in the so-called Kuwaiti theatre of operations at close to half-a-million men. But by the time the ground war started, a large part of this army was either dead or had simply melted away. Those who stayed, offered only perfunctory resistance. Iraq's air defences were poorly handled; its air force largely chose to avoid the fight; and its navy, some units of which did at least put to sea, was totally destroyed. Iraq was in every sense out-classed. Its army was poorly trained for modern manoeuvre-warfare. It faced professional opponents equipped with the very best military technology. Saddam Hussein's "fortress Kuwait" became a trap of his own making.

Iraq's performance will not become a subject of study in military academies throughout the world. In contrast, General Schwarzkopf provided a bravura performance. With its air force on the ground and no access to any intelligence beyond what its front line troops could see, Iraqi commanders had no way of knowing where the main Allied attack would fall. Regular references in Allied briefings to the possibility of an amphibious landing, helped to convince the Iraqis that the principal thrust would come against Kuwait itself. They were totally unprepared for the speed and scale of the out-flanking manoeuvre, and a significant part of Iraq's armoured reserves were caught before they could retreat northwards. Nonetheless Iraqi forces did escape. There were those who argued that the fighting should have been prolonged for one or two days so that more of Iraq's heavy equipment could be destroyed. The speed with which Iraq's vanquished army was able to turn itself around and deal with the Kurdish and Shi'ite rebellions - a task for which professionally and temperamentally it was much better suited - gave a depressing air of incompleteness to what seemed a total victory.

On the Allied side, the war demonstrated the virtues of the existing NATO war-fighting doctrine. Air-land battle, devised for the plains of northern Germany, transferred well to the sands of the Arabian desert. The coalition operated well together; its principles drawing upon years of experience of joint exercises and training. High technology played its part and not just in terms of killing: although so-called smart weapons came of age during the Gulf conflict, equally impressive was the elaborate system of command and control that guided Allied operations. It is remarkable that there were no mid-air collisions during the whole of the air campaign, despite there being hundreds of aircraft in the air at any one time.

It was a German general during World War II who described the desert as a "tactician's dream" and a "quartermaster's nightmare". And if there was one factor that underpinned the allied success in *Desert Shield* and *Desert Storm*, it was logistics. This was a war won by the warehousemen, the stock-handlers and the crew-chiefs. Some 80 per cent of Allied equipment and supplies had to come by sea; and once in Saudi Arabia, it had to be distributed to supply dumps and individual units. Whatever the qualities of the fighting soldiers, it was the logistics experts who helped to put *Desert Shield* in place, and who kept the tracks of *Desert Storm* rolling.

Jonathan Marcus
Defence Correspondent
BBC World Service

PART ONE

SHIFTING SANDS

IRAQ'S invasion and annexation of Kuwait drew together a number of historical threads. First, was the geopolitical importance of the Middle East as a source of tension in world politics: the Arab/Israeli conflict; religious orientations within Islam; and growing inequalities between Arabs, in particular between the oil-rich Arabian peninsula and the other, more densely populated countries which, even if they have oil, face complex problems of development.

Then again, many states in the Middle East are relatively new and arbitrary creations, shaped by the interplay between imperialism and various nationalisms, including Pan-Arabism. Also, the European Powers had created a contradictory situation in the Middle East after World War I: the Balfour Declaration promised the Jews a homeland in Palestine, while support for the Arab Revolt gave the Arabs reason to believe that they would achieve their national aspirations.

European contact with the Gulf goes back a long way, to the first Portuguese traders in the region. By the eighteenth century, Britain had naval supremacy in the area, and by the nineteenth Britain had established its authority in many Gulf sheikhdoms, the so-called Trucial States, together with Bahrain, with its particularly close ties to Britain and Kuwait which, though nominally Ottoman, was essentially autonomous under the al-Sabahs. The British were principally concerned with the defence of India by sea; their interest extended into the hinterland only when upheavals there threatened stability.

Formation of Iraq and Iran

In Persia, Britain had more at stake. The buffer between the Russian and Indian Empires, the country was divided at the end of the nineteenth century into spheres of interest, the British taking the southeastern, and Russia the north, including Tehran in Persia. The Russian Revolution ended the threat of a carve-up, but for a time seemed to leave Persia at the mercy of Britain. British territorial ambitions came to an end in 1921 when Reza Khan, an officer in the Russian Cossack Brigade, staged a coup d'etat and

" The world should forget a place called the Emirate of Kuwait ... "

IRAQI INFORMATION
MINISTER LATIF JASIM

established the dynasty that finally collapsed after the Islamic Revolution led by the Ayatollah Khomeini in January 1979.

Iraq was formed from the three Ottoman districts of Basra, Baghdad and Mosul, all occupied by the British in 1918. There was no historical or cultural justification for the new state. While Basra and Baghdad had links, Mosul was populated primarily by Kurds, who wanted to be part of a separate Kurdish state. Mosul, however, was important to British plans for Iraq because it gave strategic protection against nationalist and revolutionary activity to the north and east and, with its oil, offered a way to make the new state solvent. Iraq thus reflected British interests and concerns rather than the national aspirations of its peoples. Nevertheless, in 1920, the League of Nations created Iraq under a British mandate.

To understand the Arab world, we need to realize that Arab society is varied and complex. Organized in units of families and tribes, it is a flexible society in which the tribe functions well in a range of economic activities from nomadic pastoralism to urban trade and commerce, from peasant farming to fishing and seafaring. The structure of society helps to shape the concept of power. In the West we think of power as territorial, but in a tribal society, territory belongs to the tribe as a corporate entity, and power and authority grows out of relationships between people. In the twentieth century, territorial ideas of power have been laid over tribal notions without displacing them.

Oil Power

In the conservative states of the Gulf, oil revealed another concept of power: there was no distinction between the revenues of the ruling family and those of the state. In Kuwait, as elsewhere, oil revenues belong to the ruler and his family. Put another way, Kuwait can be seen as the al-Sabah's family business. And a highly profitable business it has been. It is thought that Kuwaitis own £100 billion in foreign assets and that the Kuwait Investment Office holds and manages about £30 billion of the Emir's personal fortune. All of this, ultimately, has derived from oil.

It is hard to realize that the Arabian Peninsula was extremely poor without oil. Pockets of comparative prosperity existed in coastal towns such as Jeddah, Bahrain, Kuwait, and Basra, but until they began to pump oil, the countries of the Gulf had chronically undeveloped economies. Levels of production and consumption were low; exports consisted of a limited range of products, primarily agricultural. Hunger, if not famine, was a part of existence, especially for nomads. One solution to the shortfall was raiding, not only other nomads but towns as well. Raiding was a distinctive feature of desert life, an integral part of the economy. The Iraqis, in a sense, followed this tradition when they invaded Kuwait.

Merchants have always played a central role in Arab society. In contrast to the West, trade is a respected, indeed, an honoured activity. The aristocracy of ancient merchant families often formed the backbone of the ruler's power until oil revenues made him independent. The payment of subsidies, at the same time, brought the nomads to heel. Oil revenues

Saddam Hussein personified as the peace lover in one of thousands of images that can be seen all over Iraq.

thus freed rulers from both their urban and nomadic supporters, transforming them into autocrats. It was to these autocracies that the West looked, politically and economically. To maintain them in power, it sold arms, something that would later come to haunt them.

The arming of Iraq

Arming Iraq on a scale which gave it, on paper, the fourth largest army in the world, was the work of a number of interested parties: first, the arms manufacturers and dealers who arrange the sales and whose activities are overseen by politicians with their eyes firmly fixed on balance of payments figures; second, the security services whose attention has been held by Cold War equations of world power and who regard the Middle East as a theatre of operations; and finally, the autocrats for whom strong armies are primarily designed to quell internal dissent.

With the discovery of oil new powers entered the arena: the oil companies and the United States. Oil from Persia began to flow in commercial quantities in 1912. Iraq followed in 1927, then came Bahrain in 1933 and Saudi Arabia in 1937. World War II brought a halt to development and a cut-back in production until 1944. Kuwait began producing in 1946, followed by Qatar in 1949 and the United Arab Emirates in 1962. Iran remained the region's largest producer until 1951 when Mossadeq nationalized Anglo-Iranian and the British organized a boycott of Iranian oil. The boycott was spectacularly successful: Iran's production fell from 32,260,000 metric tons in 1950 to 1,360,000 metric tons in 1952. Iran never recovered its position as the region's major producer, having lost it to Saudi Arabia.

Kuwait's position is interesting. After 1946, its production rose steeply. In the space of two years, it had surpassed and doubled Iraq's production. Since the late 1970s production levels for the older and larger producers - Saudi Arabia, Iran, Iraq and Kuwait - declined until they reached approximately half their earlier maximum levels. In the case of Kuwait, the decline was even steeper, to about one-third of maximum. The reason for this is not a

drop in demand but the coming on-stream of alternative sources of supply

It is remarkable how successful the oil companies have been in preserving their control despite the political disruption. This is partly because they have stuck together in a crisis, and have remained highly profitable enterprises despite having to share the profits more equitably with the producer states, and more recently, to accept nationalization of the oil fields and refineries.

Though the Organization of Oil Producing Countries (OPEC) became in the 1970s a model for primary producers attempting to exercise control over prices, its career has been chequered. The five founder members - Iraq, Saudi Arabia, Iran, Kuwait and Venezuela - created OPEC in 1960 to regulate petroleum prices by agreement among themselves. Inevitably, OPEC became political, debating issues beyond prices, including production and nationalization. In June 1971, it agreed that members should seek 20 percent stakes in their concessionary companies, rising to 51 percent. Some countries pursued this policy eagerly; others, the conservative Arab states, hesitated. Only in 1972, led by Saudi Arabia, did they open negotiations. With the Yom Kippur War and the "oil crisis", the pace of nationalization quickened until, in 1980, even Saudi Arabia had taken total control of ARAMCO.

It was not until 1982 that OPEC attempted to control supply by imposing production limits on its members. This

THE CHANGING FACE OF THE MIDDLE EAST

The Middle East is a mix of races where wealth, history, geography, politics and religion have all played an equal part in changing the political boundaries of the Arabian Peninsula over the last 100 years.

LEGEND   BRITISH   FRENCH   ITALIAN

has proved difficult to implement. Non-OPEC producers, not subject to the controls, and even members, particularly Iran, over-produced. Over-production by Kuwait and the United Arab Emirates (UAE) was one of Iraq's grievances in the period before the invasion of Kuwait.

The Gulf Sheikhdoms

The history of the Gulf has thus been shaped by the region's strategic importance and by oil.

In the more recent past three strands have intersected: European, especially British, imperialism; Cold War diplomacy; and the Arab-Israeli conflict. In the history of the end of the British Empire, the sheikhdoms of the Gulf are unique. Of them it could be said that they

did not seek independence, but had it thrust upon them.

Perched on the edge of Arabia, with more powerful neighbours all around, they sheltered under the umbrella of British power until the late 1960s. Their fear of independence was well founded: the oil resources of Oman and the UAE were only just emerging.

Both Iran and Saudi Arabia posed major threats, each claiming some or all of their territory: the sheikhdoms had substantial populations of Shi'ites, many of whom were of Persian origin, while Saudi Arabia had claims to Bahrain and the desert hinterlands of Kuwait and Abu Dhabi. In addition, Iraq claimed Kuwait.

Britain took a severe knock in the Suez Crisis in 1956. Having lost control of the

Suez Canal, it attempted to maintain itself in the East by securing the British naval base at Aden through the creation, early in 1963, of the Federation of South Arabia, but the scheme was shattered by Egyptian intervention.

So long as Britain maintained a presence east of Suez, the Gulf sheikhdoms were secure enough. But in the 1960s, Britain's economy was under severe strain, and the government was planning cuts in defence expenditure. In 1967, the British government decided to make savings by abandoning the Gulf: it was announced that the sheikhdoms would become independent in March 1971.

Cold War diplomacy

Whereas the British took the view that their interests, even after 1956, were best served by maintaining their own military presence east of Suez, Washington's position, very much determined by its Cold War obsessions, was that its interests could best be defended by establishing unity of interest with a local autocrat - the "regional superpower". In the Gulf, the Americans focused on Iran and Saudi Arabia; after the Iranian Revolution, the focus shifted to Iraq. The collapse of British power after the Suez Crisis posed serious problems for the United States. In 1957, the Eisenhower Doctrine extended to the Middle East the pledge to assist any state threatened by communism, and in 1958 CENTO was formed. The real threat came from Arab nationalism: Nasserism. In July 1958, Washington acted to prevent coups in Jordan and the Lebanon, with US Marines wading ashore on Beirut's beaches. For its part, the Soviet Union intervened increasingly in the Middle East, supporting "leftist" regimes with arms, and taking up the anti-Israeli stance of Arab states.

Arab-Israeli conflict

In the minds of most Arabs, however, it was the Arab-Israeli conflict which was crucial. It is not possible to understand events in this region without looking at this immensely important issue. From its birth on 14 May 1948, Israel has been at war with its neighbours. Within days of its formation the Arabs attacked, with disastrous consequences for themselves.

Although small in size, Kuwait is a major producer and exporter of oil and petroleum-based products. Prior to the invasion Kuwait's oil reserves were 97.1 million barrels. Her GNP was $13,680 per capita, compared to Iraq's reserves of 100 million barrels and GNP of $1,960.

Contrary to expectations, the forces of the Arab League were defeated and Israel was able both to expand its territory and to "cleanse" itself of 900,000 of the approximately 1.3 million Palestinians who lived in the battle zone. The Arab intervention was a catastrophe for the Palestinian people; it also revealed how hollow had been claims of Arab unity and how ineffectual the Arab League was. Since 1948, the majority of Palestinians have lived in exile, often in refugee camps; others have made homes in other Arab countries where, as events in Kuwait have shown, they are highly vulnerable.

The Suez Crisis produced a flowering of Arab nationalism. There were moves towards a politically united Arabia and, in 1964, the PLO was formed as an umbrella for Palestinian organizations. In May, 1967, Nasser ordered out of Sinai the UN troops stationed there since Suez. He then closed the Straits of Tiran, at the mouth of the Red Sea, to Israeli shipping. On 5 June, Israel launched a pre-emptive attack on Egypt and Syria which, in the course of six days, gave them the Golan Heights, the West Bank and Sinai. It was a second catastrophe for the Palestinians and a terrible blow to Arab pride. It also marked the defeat of "progressive" nationalist thinking and made way for the dominance of "conservatism", represented by Saudi Arabia and by Islamic fundamentalism. The 1973 Yom Kippur war merely reinforced these trends, while oil made the conservatives even more powerful. To the humiliating defeat at Israel's hands must be added the frustration of many poor Arabs of becoming a cheap, "foreign", labour supply for their rich neighbours.

Oil has created immense inequalities in Arab society: as the plight of the Palestinians became more desperate, Kuwait was reckoned to have the highest per capita GNP in the world. The conservative Arab states have ignored the plight of workers within their own countries and the larger problems of population growth and food supply. They have ignored the development problems of the region and instead have invested heavily in world financial markets, especially in the West, in petro-chemical installations, and in ostentatious public works such as airports and palaces.

Iran-Iraq war

Though the Iran-Iraq War was about regional power, much of the struggle was for specific objectives, control of the Shatt-al-Arab in particular. (The waterway is formed by the confluence of the Tigris and Euphrates and flows into the northern tip of the Gulf. The east bank is the historical border between Iran and Iraq. In contrast to many Middle Eastern

"Iraq's battle will extend to the whole world..."

PRESIDENT SADDAM HUSSEIN

boundaries, it is fixed and recognized.)

Initially, Iraq made a number of gains. But by the end of 1980, the offensive was over and Iraq settled down to a protracted war of defence in which it lost all the territory it had gained by the time of the ceasefire. The war was long, painful and destructive, reminiscent of World War I. Yet given the range and quantity of weapons available to both sides, it is surprising how unsophisticated the military operations were. In reality, neither Iran nor Iraq was able to deploy the weapons they had purchased at such great cost. In part, this was because the overall direction of the war was in the hands of politicians rather than soldiers. It is important to remember that Saddam Hussein, who took command of the Iraqi forces, has no military training. His background is political, within the apparatus of the Ba'athist Party and the security organizations of the state.

America's role in the conflict, though confined to intelligence and maritime protection, began to grow. Such was Washington's hostility to Iran that it ignored Iraq's missile attack on the USS *Stark* in which 37 sailors died. Increasingly, the United States attacked Iranian naval targets, mainly small patrol boats operating in the Straits of Hormuz. On 3 July 1988, Iranian patrol boats fired on a US helicopter. In the fight that followed, two boats were sunk and a third damaged. A few hours later, the USS *Vincennes* shot down an Iran Air airbus, killing all 290 people on board. Another feature of the war was terrorist attacks on civilian and economic targets in Kuwait, Bahrain and Saudi Arabia, and against American targets wherever possible. The most notable of these was the bombing, on 21 December 1988, of Pan Am flight 103 in which 259 people died.

Invasion of Kuwait

The Iraqi invasion of Kuwait took place just before the second anniversary of the 20 August 1988 ceasefire in the Iran-Iraq war. The war had left Iraq politically shaken and deeply in debt. Before the war, Iraqi reserves had been £30 billion; in 1988 Baghdad owed £70 billion, half to the Gulf states, among whom Kuwait was prominent. Saddam Hussein saw Iraq as the defender of the Arab Gulf against Islamic fundamentalism, and he was angry with his neighbours for not giving more support. On top of this came the collapse in oil prices, at a time when Iraq was finding it difficult to ship its oil through the Shatt because of Iranian attacks. At the Arab League Summit in May 1990, Saddam Hussein accused some Arab producers of maintaining low prices: They were, he said, waging "economic war". In July, at the same time that OPEC assigned quotas designed to raise prices, the Iraqi Foreign Minister, Tariq Aziz, accused Kuwait of stealing from the neutral zone £1.3 billion of Iraqi oil, simultaneously writing off £5.5 billion in Kuwaiti loans to Iraq.

At the end of July, the world suddenly found itself deep in an unexpected Middle East crisis. On 24 July, Iraq moved 30,000 troops to the Kuwait border. The Egyptian President, Hosni Mubarak, visited Baghdad, Kuwait and Riyadh in an attempt to mediate. The following day, the US Ambassador to Iraq, April Glaspie, told Saddam Hussein that, "We have no opinion on the Arab-Arab conflicts like your border disagreements with Kuwait", adding, though this was not made public until much later, that she had warned Saddam that the United States would use its power to protect its friends in the Gulf. But the Iraqis were not accustomed to hearing tough talk from the Americans. Since 1979 the USA had been courting Baghdad, agreeing weapons supplies and making friendly official visits. The warning, because it was so out of character, fell on deaf ears.

On 27 July, Kuwait agreed to Iraq's demands for compensation, without giving way on claims to the islands of Bubiyan and Warba. Two days later, King Hussein of Jordan failed in his attempts to mediate. On the last day of July, at Jeddah, officials from Iraq and Kuwait met for talks which ended the following day when the Kuwaitis refused to give up the two islands and write off the Iraqi debt. By this time, Iraq had 100,000 troops poised on the border. With hindsight, it is clear that the situation had been dangerous for the last six months.

The day of the Iraqi invasion was, not surprisingly, a busy one. Within hours the action had been condemned almost universally, the UN Security Council called into emergency session and an emergency meeting of Arab League foreign ministers called in Cairo. Iraq warned the United States that if it intervened in Kuwait, the country would become a "graveyard".

By the end of the day, Iraq was in full possession of Kuwait, the Emir had fled, the major powers, including the Soviet Union, had demanded Iraq's withdrawal and the Arab League foreign ministers had postponed their discussions for a day. Syria had called for an Arab League summit, British Airways flight 149 was stranded in Kuwait, and the United States, Britain and France had frozen all Iraqi and Kuwaiti assets in their respective countries.

Thus, within 24 hours, virtually all the elements of the Gulf crisis were fixed: the complex diplomacy, in which the Soviet-American "new world order" was explored and exploited; the confusion of the Arab League and the European

Community; the formal leading role of the United Nations; and the belief of many that the crisis would see the organization fulfil the promise of peace envisaged in its charter.

There was also the brutality of the Iraqis in Kuwait, the taking of hostages,

In 1979 Shia Muslims ousted the Shah of Iran, proclaiming a Muslim Republic led by Ayatollah Khomeini. In 1980 Iran and Iraq entered into an eight year war.

and the attempt to use economic sanctions to force Iraq's withdrawal.

By the end of the first week, the Security Council resolutions 661 (6 August) and 662 (9 August) had introduced economic sanctions and had declared null and void Iraq's annexation of Kuwait. Until the end of November and the passage of Resolution 678, attention was focused on the hostages and the enforcement of the embargo.

The word "hostage" is an emotive one and the notion of many thousands of them especially powerful. Politicians on both sides were at first hesitant to use the word. Iraqi policy throughout the crisis was shortsighted and opportunistic; it seems likely that it evolved with the crisis.

BA Flight 149 literally came out of the sky; the many foreigners who became hostages were simply trapped, then detained, then became hostages and human shields. The many nationalities involved made this a subject of almost universal concern. It is easy to forget that by far the largest groups of foreigners trapped in Iraq and Kuwait were the Asian workers - Indians, Pakistanis, Bangladeshis and so on - who numbered tens of thousands. Too poor and insignificant to be taken hostage, they became refugees, pawns in the diplomacy of the crisis. They were abandoned to their own devices, living rough in the desert often without food and water. The Indian Government figured prominently in efforts to repatriate workers; in late September, they sent ships with relief supplies to Iraq. By late September and early October, refugees in large numbers were being evacuated either by sea, or overland through Jordan. The more publicized releases came with the visits to Baghdad of prominent figures such as Edward Heath, Jesse Jackson and Willy Brandt, then the announcements in Iraq that national contingents were free to go, beginning with the French on 23 October and ending on 7 December with the release of all foreigners, a week before the UN deadline.

With hindsight it seems clear that the hostages were the best defence the Iraqis had. Their willingness to release them perhaps indicates a mistaken notion that a negotiated settlement was possible. The US position was hard from the beginning - its diplomacy was not about negotiation but compliance with the UN resolutions. London operated in tandem with Washington, often playing the part of the bellicose partner. America's diplomatic objectives, effectively summarized in the series of Security Council resolutions, ignored any idea of negotiation with the Iraqis. In the only direct contact between the two, the meeting of Secretary of State Baker and Foreign Minister Aziz on 9 January in Geneva, the Americans were primarily interested in diffusing the growing international concern about the rigidity of their position. What Baker took to Geneva was yet another restatement of a consistent line: get out of Kuwait by the

15 January or else. President Bush's letter to Saddam Hussein, which the Iraqis refused to accept, was in the same vein.

There were, however, two areas in which the USA was diplomatically active. The first was its relations with the Soviet Union; the second, the negotiations necessary to secure the adoption of UN Resolution 678 on 29 November which authorized the use of force and set 15 January as the compromise deadline for withdrawal.

Iraq's position was only slightly less rigid. Its repeated stance was that its incorporation of Kuwait was not negotiable, though there were other indications, not least the looting, which suggested that the Iraqis knew they couldn't hold the territory.

But Iraq did pursue the time-honoured tradition of diplomatic negotiation when it raised the issue of linking Kuwait to Palestine. Iraqi diplomacy, however, was inconsistent and erratic. At the end of the day, Saddam Hussein had squandered the limited support of Middle East states such as Yemen, Libya, Algeria, and even Iran, which, however much it disliked the occupation of Kuwait, hated an American-led military solution even more.

Saddam's intransigence pushed his potential allies into neutrality.

Similarly, there should be no illusions about the depth of support for America's no-linkage stance. The Arab members of the coalition, notably Saudi Arabia, Egypt and Syria, would like nothing more than a conference on the Palestine question. Most non-aligned states would agree.

The Soviet Union made it clear throughout the crisis that though it would stick to its UN commitments, it favoured a more general and regional negotiating position. In some sense it was the Soviet Union which engaged in the most serious attempt to find a diplomatic solution to the crisis. All America's European allies,

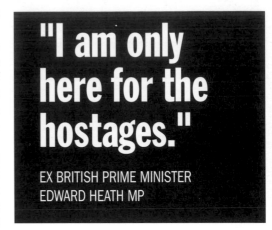

"I am only here for the hostages."

EX BRITISH PRIME MINISTER
EDWARD HEATH MP

except Britain, signalled their willingness to look at a general Middle East peace conference after Iraq withdrew.

Iraq's only consistent support came from the PLO, the state without a country. With hindsight, the Gulf War seems to have been yet another disaster for the Palestinians. But it is difficult to see what options Arafat and the PLO had except to attempt to ride the wave of the crisis, hoping to win something for themselves from Iraq's aggression and defiance.

BELOW & RIGHT: *As the Iraqis' grip on Kuwait became stronger, the flood of refugees from the country became greater.*

RIGHT: *President Bush reacted within hours to the Kuwait invasion, ordering the largest, fastest and most complicated military deployment in history.*

PART TWO

GATHERING STORM

EARLY on the morning of 2 August 1990, Iraqi troops and armour rolled across the border with Kuwait and proceeded to subjugate the small but immensely wealthy state in a matter of hours. In so doing, they precipitated a crisis the like of which had not been seen for many years, for within 48 hours of the invasion, no fewer than 100,000 Iraqi soldiers were reported to be gathering on Kuwait's southern border with Saudi Arabia.

Iraq's President Saddam Hussein quickly went on record to deny that he had any territorial ambitions in Saudi Arabia, but in the light of previous statements by Hussein, this denial was viewed with scepticism at best and scorn at worst. Faced with the possibility of attack, the government in Riyadh quickly recognized that it had little chance of effectively defending itself, and it wasted no time in turning to the outside world - and to the USA in particular - for assistance. What followed was one of the most extra-ordinary military build-ups that the world has ever seen.

Objectives

Accomplished under United Nations auspices, this massive infusion of military might had two broad objectives. The first was to forestall the possibility of invasion, an objective that was satisfied fairly rapidly. The second - which took much longer to achieve - was to assemble sufficient resources to initiate offensive operations against Iraq, with a view to liberating Kuwait.

Once Saudi Arabia had asked for help, the various nations that were eventually to form the Allied coalition wasted little or no time in sending men and *matériel*. The US contribution, under the rather grandiose code name *Desert Shield,* was easily the largest and eventually numbered over 400,000 personnel drawn from all branches of the US armed forces. This contribution, along with other elements of the multinational coalition force, was placed under the overall control of US Army General Norman Schwarzkopf in his capacity as Commander-in-Chief, Central Command, the agency responsible for all US military forces in the Middle East.

It was that agency that was ultimately given the task of developing battle plans for the liberation of Kuwait, but the most urgent consideration in early August was to forestall further Iraqi excursions into foreign territory. In consequence, the build-up was spearheaded by an infusion of air power, since this could reach the theatre quickly and become operational in the shortest time. First to head east across the Atlantic were nearly 50 F-15C Eagle air superiority fighters of the 1st Tactical Fighter Wing. These left Langley

"If force is necessary it will be quick, massive and decisive."

US VICE-PRESIDENT DAN QUAYLE

AFB, Virginia, on 7 August and flew nonstop to Dhahran, Saudi Arabia with the aid of no fewer than seven in-flight refuellings. Within hours of arrival, they were mounting combat air patrols along the northern border with Iraq and Iraqi occupied Kuwait.

More American fighters followed, and by the end of August a substantial proportion of US Air Force resources had gathered at a number of desert bases in various Gulf states, with much of this initial equipment provided by Tactical Air Command (TAC) and the United States Air Forces in Europe (USAFE). F-16 Fighting Falcons had moved to Sharjah and Doha; F-15E Strike Eagles were at Thumrait; A-10A Thunderbolt 11 tank-busters had arrived at Al Jubayl;F-lll interdiction/-strike aircraft had shifted to Turkey and Saudi Arabia; and the much vaunted but still largely unproven F-117A "Stealth"

fighter was at an unknown base in Saudi Arabia.

"Heavier metal" was also on the move, with Strategic Air Command (SAC) B-52G Stratofortress bombers and KC-135 in-flight refuelling tankers deploying to various locations in and around the Gulf, while RC135 "ferrets" and high-flying TR-lAs set about the mission of gathering vital intelligence.

Britain's response to the Saudi call for assistance was almost as rapid, Defence Minister Tom King announcing on 9 August that Jaguar strike fighters and Tornado interceptors would be sent as the initial contingent of the rather more prosaically named *Operation Granby.* Within three days, a dozen examples of each type had departed from British bases, the Jaguars going first to Oman and eventually to Bahrain, while the Tornados headed for Dhahran, from where they very quickly took responsibility for a share of the round-the-clock air defence requirement. Within a matter of weeks, more hardware followed in the shape of Tornado interdictor/strike aircraft; and the RAF tactical contingent was eventually to rise to more than 70 aircraft plus numerous support helicopters, tankers and transports.

Ground forces

As the initial air elements were settling into their new quarters, the first of several hundred thousand troops were en route to the region, accompanied by countless tons of equipment. Again, it was the USA that led the way, with soldiers of the 82nd Airborne Division being airlifted from Fort Bragg, North Carolina, nonstop to Dhahran, Riyadh and Thumrait aboard C-5 Galaxies and C-141 Starlifters of the USAF's Military Airlift Command (MAC). For the latter agency, the ensuing months were a period of intense activity as more and more soldiers moved to the Gulf

A C-5 Galaxy from MAC taxies into Dhahran at the beginning of the Desert Shield *build up in early August 1990. On board elements of the US Army's 82nd Airborne prepare to disembark.*

along with a considerable amount of heavy equipment, including tanks and other types of armoured fighting vehicle (AFV), helicopters and the myriad support equipment that is required by ground forces engaged in battle. Indeed, the burden placed on MAC soon necessitated mobilization of part of the Civil Reserve Air Fleet (CRAF), with suitably configured commercial transport

> # "...he is up against a foe he can't possibly manage"
>
> US PRESIDENT GEORGE BUSH

airports and air bases throughout the Gulf as the build-up continued.

Still more *matériel* arrived by ship, Gulf ports quickly reaching near-saturation point as vast quantities of military paraphernalia flooded in, courtesy of the Military Sealift Command, aboard a fleet of chartered cargo vessels. That, of course, was only part of the picture, for still more ships were disgorging cargo for use by other ground forces from other nations.

Britain was one of those nations, committing an eventual total of about 40,000 soldiers to the United Nations force. In the vanguard was the 7th Armoured Brigade, which began to move to the Gulf from Germany just before the end of September, along with its Chieftain main battle tanks, supporting AFVs and artillery pieces, as well as an air component made up of Lynx and Gazelle helicopters. A few weeks later, the 4th Armoured Brigade followed.

How the "Screaming Eagles" went to war

At 06.30 hrs on Friday 10 August 1990 the 101st Airborne Division (Air Assault), the only Air Assault Division in the world, received orders to depart for Saudi Arabia on operation *Desert Shield*.. As part of the US Army's Rapid Deployment Force (RDF), the Division is trained to fight worldwide including in the desert. In 1980 elements of the Division participated in the rapid-deployment joint task force exercise *Bright Star* near Cairo,Egypt; and several times each year elements of the Division undertake training exercises in the Mojave Desert. As part of the US Army's RDF, the Division is capable of deployment by air, land or sea and has a battalion-size unit ready to deploy within 12 hours, and a brigade-size force ready within 18 hours.

Within hours of their order to move over 17,000 soldiers, together with their weapons,vehicles and the Division's fleet of 400 helicopters, began to move by air and sea to the northwest sector of Saudi Arabia near Hafar al-Batin, close to the border with Iraq. USAF C-5A Galaxy and C-141 Starlifter aircraft spent over a week flying in and out of Campbell Army Airfield, Kentucky, helping to deploy the Division. The 101st, along with 160th Special Operations Aviation Regiment (Task Force 160), who are also resident at Campbell Army Airfield, regularly practise the loading of their helicopters aboard USAF transport aircraft as part of their RDF role. The airlift for Desert Shield eclipsed the previous record for a rapid deployment which took place in December 1967 when the Division moved from Fort Campbell to Bien Hoa, Vietnam

The 101st Airborne had been training for such a role since they exchanged their parachutes for helicopters and took on the air assault role in 1974. Unlike the airmobile concept - the transportation of forces by air from one location to another - air assault Is a combined arms concept, divisional in strength, with its own infantry, antitank, support and aviation brigades. This provides a self-contained, highly mobile force, capable of movement by air and able to fight on the ground, supported by air reconnaissance and attack helicopters. The Division's aviation assets include the AH-64A Apache, AH-IF Cobra, UH-60 Black Hawk, OH-58C/D Kiowas and the CH-47D Chinook. The Division is ideally suited to attacking armoured forces and can quickly reinforce key positions or conduct deep strike missions. The mobility provided by their helicopters allows the Division to mass,disperse and recycle forces rapidly throughout a huge battle area. They can be used for screening, covering force and delay operations. The Division is

well trained for night operations with aircrews experienced in night vision goggle/non-illuminated night flying techniques. Every item of battlefield equipment belonging to the Division is capable of being flown in or under its helicopters.

Images of the 101st Airborne Division (Air Assault) training at Fort Campbell, Kentucky. The ten-day training programme that a potential recruit has to go through to earn his Air Assault wings is known as the "ten toughest days in the world".

Still more troops, from Arab states such as Egypt and Syria as well as from France, were also committed to the Allied cause in considerable quantities as Saudi Arabia quickly grew to resemble a huge armed camp.

Allied naval blockade

While extensive use was made of shipping to transfer the vast stockpiles of resources that would be needed to successfully wage war on Iraq, maritime activity was by no means confined to the

"I believe a land war is inevitable"

BRITISH C-IN-C LT- GENERAL
SIR PETER DE LA BILLIERE

mere movement of hardware, for a multinational contingent of warships was soon assembled in the Persian Gulf and the Red Sea. Indeed, it was at sea that one could best observe the true nature of the multinational effort, with Australian, British, Canadian, Dutch, French, Italian and US warships amongst the armada that was vital in implementing the naval blockade: just one aspect of UN efforts to isolate Iraq and force it to comply with Security Council resolutions.

US aircraft carriers

Almost inevitably, it was the American contribution that was dominant and as far as US involvement was concerned, the largest and most visible warships must surely have been the aircraft carriers, which began to head towards the Gulf within a couple of days of the call for assistance being received.

With the exception of the USS *Midway,* each of these warships accommodated in the region of 80-85 aircraft, including pure fighters like the F-14 Tomcat,

From the Falklands to the Gulf

As the senior of the the two Front-Line (845/846) Commando Squadrons, 846 Naval Air Squadron is permanently at 72-hour notice to deploy worldwide on operational tasks. The Squadron was confident of an early role in *Operation Granby/Desert Shield* and this confidence proved correct.

The Squadron's primary role is to provide eight Sea King HC4s in support of 3 Commando Brigade Royal Marines,specifically on the northern flank of NATO in northern Norway ,but also worldwide in a variety of roles. 846 Squadron played an important role in the Falklands (1982) conflict and was the first British helicopter squadron to use night vision goggles (NVG) on operational missions, inserting and extracting Special Forces units on night missions. In 1984 the Squadron supported British forces in Beirut, which included assisting in the evacuation of British and Commonwealth civilians from the British Embassy in West Beirut. In October 1987 the Squadron was called upon to provide an aircraft to support minesweeping activities in the Persian Gulf during operation 'Cimnel'. Having completed their four months deployment to Arctic Norway, the Squadron deployed several of their Sea King helicopters to Egypt in April/May 1990 for a major desert training exercise with Egyptian forces.

As the Gulf crisis escalated, UN sanctions against Iraq were imposed and these required policing. The Royal Navy began to reinforce their existing Armilla Patrol, which had been in the Gulf for over 10 years, and to increase their warship presence. On 22 August 1990 two 846 Squadron Sea Kings, along with 30 aircrew and maintainers, embarked aboard the RFA *Fort Grange* , a Fleet Replenishment Ship, to undertake the Helicopter Delivery Service (HDS) Flight in support of RN ships operating in the Gulf. These were the first British support helicopters to fly operationally during *Operation Granby.*

By early September the Squadron was put on seven days notice to move. RFA *Argus* began her conversion to a Primary Casualty Receiving Ship including a 100 bed hospital. RFA *Argus* entered service in 1989 as an Aviation Training Ship and for her hospital role, she would operate four Sea King helicopters off her five-spot landing deck. As British

land forces began to deploy to Saudi Arabia the need for such a hospital ship increased. By early October, 846 Squadron was tasked to provide four of their remaining six helicopters to the Maritime Casevac role to be based aboard the RFA *Argus.* The Squadron was also to be ready to deploy ashore in support of land-based forces should this be necessary. On 4 October, the Squadron received a preliminary departure date, and the first of their helicopters was painted in desert camouflage colours by 15 October.

Over the next few weeks aircrew and maintainers undertook refresher training in NBC warfare, testing their respirators and equipment. Pilots undertook refresher training missions wearing their aviator AR5 respirators, learning how to take on fluids while wearing night vision goggles etc. Other activities included zeroing-in the sights of their personnel weapons, fitting newly issued PLJs (personnel life jackets/load carrying jerkins) and Kevlar body armour and making up desert aircrew survival packs.

On Sunday 28 October four "Pink" 846 Squadron Sea Kings departed their home base at RNAS Yeovilton in Somerset and flew in formation across Dartmoor to RFA *Argus* lying at anchor in Plymouth Sound. *Argus* sailed early on 29 October but had to return later that night with steering problems. Once repaired, she finally set off on 31 October, arriving on station in the Gulf on 15 November.

The Squadron spent much of the transit time in working crews up to operational readiness. For their Gulf role the helicopters had received newly arrived operational enhancement equipment, which needed to be fitted. Squadron pilots had little time to learn the capabilities of the ship and how best to use the new enhancements. These included the fitting of sand filters, NAVSTAR Global Positioning System (GPS), a comprehensive Defence Aids Suite, an improved communications fit, and fitting 7.62mm door guns. Later fits included an updated TANS 2 (Super TANS). All the crews required work-up on this equipment. They had to practise day and night deck landings and night vision goggle flying techniques at sea. They were also to be the first squadron to fly multiple helicopter night vision goggle operations from RFA *Argus.*

ABOVE: RFA Argus *sits in Plymouth Harbour awaiting the flight of 846 Squadron helicopters from RNAS Yeovilton. Shortly after they landed* Argus *hove to and set out for the Gulf.* BELOW: *Arming up small arms and checking equipment was an important part of the pre-operational work-up at Yeovilton.*

BELOW: *A distinctive look is given to any pilot who wears Night Vision Goggles and these are the latest type, used for the first time by pilots from 846.*

ABOVE: *Heading toward Plymouth Sound where RFA* Argus *is waiting, the crew of these HC4 Sea Kings take a last look at the green lush countryside below them.*

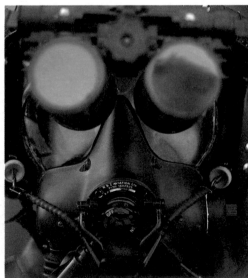

RIGHT: *In her operational habitat at last,* Argus *runs at full speed through the waters of the northern Gulf. One of 846's Sea Kings hovers ahead.*

dedicated attack aircraft such as the A-6 Intruder and the multimission-capable F/A-18 Hornet, plus E-2C Hawkeyes for early warning/control, S-3 Vikings and SH-3 Sea Kings for anti-submarine warfare, and EA-6B Prowlers for electronic countermeasure tasks. Between them, the six carriers that constituted the peak strength of the US Navy contribution could muster between 450 and 500 aircraft and helicopters of all types, making this contingent a formidable force in its own right.

That was by no means the end of the US Navy force, which also included numerous surface combatants. Most spectacular in terms of sheer firepower were the battleships *Wisconsin* and *Missouri* and their heavy guns, while Tomahawk cruise missiles were to play a key part once battle was joined in mid-January. Other naval assets consisted of a number of assault ships carrying Marine Corps helicopters and AV-8B Harrier II attack aircraft as well as ground forces specializing in assault from the sea.

BELOW & RIGHT:*The Royal Saudi Army is a highly trained,volunteer force. Lined up on the Saudi-Kuwaiti border this tank crew man specially modifed French AMX-30S MBTs.*

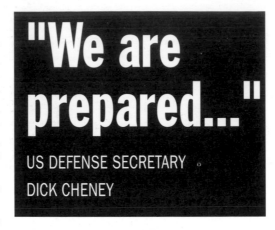

"We are prepared..."
US DEFENSE SECRETARY DICK CHENEY

Two Marine Expeditionary Forces were eventually transferred to the Gulf area and some of the troops assigned to them were among the first to arrive in Saudi Arabia, courtesy of MAC and the CRAF.

Once the threat of an Iraqi invasion receded, a more leisurely transfer was effected, with later elements coming by sea along with their own heavy equipment and that for the early arrivals. Ultimately, the best part of half a dozen Marine Expeditionary Brigades were relocated to the Middle East. Many went ashore, but some constituted the fighting element of an amphibious task force, used to bluff the Iraqi military command into diverting precious resources to defend against an assault from the sea which never came.

Organic Marine air power was also dispatched to the Gulf in large numbers, and eventually totalled about 300 aircraft and helicopters which arrived between August and November 1990. At least six F/A-18 Hornet fighter-attack squadrons were amongst the Marine Corps tactical air component, along with A-6E Intruders (one squadron), AV-8B Harrier IIs (four squadrons), EA-6B Prowlers (one squadron) and AH-IW Sea Cobra helicopter gunships (four squadrons). Deployment methods varied, with some units flying direct from stateside bases while others were ferried to the region aboard amphibious vessels. Movement of supporting personnel was accomplished with the aid of MAC and the CRAF as well as Military Sealift Command and the service's own small force of transport aircraft, which was also pressed into service in the in-flight refuelling role.

By 16 January 1991, when the UN deadline for an Iraqi withdrawal expired, the air component was ready and primed for action. Within hours, *Desert Shield* metamorphosed into *Desert Storm* with the launching of the air offensive. Even then, some ground forces had still to arrive, but they were in place and ready to move at 0400 hours on 24 February when coalition forces began their push into Iraq and Kuwait...

RIGHT: *The first contingent of Britain's 7th Armoured Brigade Challenger MBTs head ashore from the dockside at Damman.*

PART THREE

DESERT STORM

UN Secretary General fails to convince Saddam of peace wish

The day before the first attacks of *Desert Storm* was quiet. In Baghdad, journalists found the streets as deserted as those of Kuwait City shown on Iraqi television as Saddam Hussein toured on the eve of the deadline.

The mosques were packed; the lights of the city were blazing. No preparations for the defence of the city or its population were apparent. Ironically, it was Israel, fearful of chemical attack, which seemed most ready for war. Schools were closed, curfews imposed in Palestinian areas, gas masks distributed.

There was a flurry of last minute appeals for peace. The French initiative, too late and too complex, came to nothing. Pérez de Cuéllar appealed to Saddam Hussein to "turn the course of events away from catastrophe", promising action on the Arab-Israeli conflict and safe conduct for Iraqi troops out of Kuwait.

The die was cast: Bush was ready to make the tough decisions ahead when necessary. The Iraqis staged pro-Saddam rallies and to an American journalist's question about Kuwait, replied: "Would you pull out of California? Kuwait is our territory..."

Many people went to church to pray and the anti-war demonstrations became vigils. Coalition troops continued their training and air crews still mounted their round-the-clock combat air patrols. Some wrote letters home. They all waited.

It was a quiet day, in which the world made itself ready for war.

J PEREZ DE CUELLAR

Javier Pérez de Cuéllar is a Peruvian diplomat who became the UN's fifth secretary general in 1982 in succession to Kurt Waldheim of Austria. He was re-elected to serve a second five-year term in 1987.

Pérez de Cuéllar was born in Lima in 1920, took a law degree at the Catholic University of Lima, and joined Peru's diplomatic service in 1944. His early postings were to France, the UK, Bolivia and Brazil; he subsequently served in departmental posts within the Peruvian ministry of external relations, and as ambassador to the USSR, Poland, Switzerland, and Venezuela. His UN experience has included service as Peru's permanent representative and various special appointments within the Secretariat.

Anti-war protests in Germany. Massive peace movement afoot in Europe

Germany saw some of its largest peace demonstrations as tens of thousands of people took to the streets in cities and also blockaded US military bases.

Unlike many previous peace marches the entire spectrum of the population was present, both young and old. According to opinion polls over 80 percent of Germans oppose the use of force in the Gulf.

In France, thousands went to the National Assembly in Paris to protest. At the same time the French Prime Minister, Michel Rocard, was stating that the 12,000 French troops in the Gulf would be placed under US control - but only for a limited period.

In Bangladesh there were clashes in Dhakar between supporters of Saddam Hussein and Bengalis who had recently been repatriated from Kuwait after the August invasion.

The United Nations has been debating the situation of Iraq until the small hours. The tensions of the moment show to dramatic effect on the face of the Secretary General, seen here in conversation in New York at a Security Council Debate some 24 hours before the deadline expired.

PRESIDENT

The Hawk anti-aircraft missile system is deployed by both the US Marines and the Army in Saudi Arabia. It has been used by Israel for a number of years as a front-line defensive missile. It proved highly effective in the 1973 war, downing some 20 or more Egyptian and Syrian aircraft.

Day 1

Wednesday 16 January

The UN deadline expires at midnight UN time (0500 GMT), and the UN and its allies are now authorized to use all measures necessary to force Iraq out of Kuwait. President Bush is said by the White House to be "at peace with himself, and ready to take the decisions that would have to be made".

Saddam Hussein takes direct control of Iraqi armed forces, a formality to emphasize that the country is on a war footing.

In the US the FBI is ordered to track down some three thousand Iraqis whose visas have expired.

British Prime Minister, John Major, gives a briefing on the impending attack to Opposition leader Neil Kinnock, Liberal Democratic Leader Paddy Ashdown, and former Prime Minister Edward Heath. He then informs the Queen.

President Bush issues the order to attack through the national command authority.

At 2150 GMT, cruise missiles are launched from warships in the Gulf marking the opening of the Allied attack.

At around 2330 GMT (0230 Iraqi time 17 January 1991), heavy anti-aircraft fire is reported in Baghdad.

World worries if war breaks out

There are voices raised all over the world at the impending threat of war.

China, in a signed statement from her official News Agency, issued a stern warning to the United States government that it should not rush to war and in the Vatican Pope Paul II offered up prayers, appealing at the same time for Saddam Hussein to make a generous gesture of peace and avoid war.

It was Israel who feared the most today, with reports of a build up of forces on the Jordanian and Syrian borders. "We are in a state of war" said David Levy, the Foreign Minister. As a result Israel put curfew restrictions on Palestinians living in the Gaza Strip, reserved space for casualties and closed schools. The Air Force was placed on the highest state of alert and a communiqué said that the Israeli Air Force would have no hesitation in chasing Iraqi aircraft over the air space of Jordan and Syria. If Israel was attacked, Prime Minister Yitzhak Shamir firmly stated that it would respond and "hit back firmly and strongly".

The mood throughout the country was nervous, knowing that the inevitable would happen sooner rather than later. Most of the Israeli people were pinning hopes on the American and Saudi AWACs (Early Warning Airborne System) and satellite monitoring to warn them of impending air or missile strikes from Iraq.

Both Patriot and Hawk missiles are in place awaiting immediate launch should the signal come. There is doubt that the recently deployed Patriot missile system is ready as the Israeli crews are still undergoing instruction from American experts, but the Hawk *is* proven in battle and pointed menacingly at the clear blue skies overlooking the Jordan Valley.

Warplanes bomb Baghdad: "the liberation of Kuwait has begun" announces White House

"And gentlemen in England now a-bed shall think themselves accursed they were not here..." With those words from Shakespeare's *Henry V*, Air Commodore Ian Macfadyen presided over the final briefing before RAF aircrew went into action. Outside, their aircraft were bombed up and ready to go, as *Desert Shield* evolved into *Desert Storm*.

Similar scenes undoubtedly took place at a host of other air bases throughout the Gulf as the Allied air forces made ready for war. The brunt of the initial air assault and of the sustained bombing operations that followed, was borne by the USA, flying from land bases as well as aircraft carriers in the Red Sea and the Gulf. Valuable contributions were also made by the Royal Air Force, the Royal Saudi Air Force and the Free Kuwait Air Force, all of which took part in the first wave.

Objectives on that day were principally concerned with inhibiting Iraq's capacity to wage effective war; command and control facilities were near the top of the list. Many of these high value targets lay in the Iraqi capital of Baghdad, close to the seat of government and heavily defended by a mixture of antiaircraft artillery and surface-to-air missiles.

The first attacks on the capital were mainly the preserve of the much -vaunted but still relatively unproven Lockheed F-117A

British Prime Minister John Major, outside 10 Downing Street in London, announces the start of the bombing war

"Stealth Fighter" which was evidently able to operate with impunity in the night skies above Baghdad. "Stealth" soon proved its worth, early successes including an attack in which laser-guided ordnance was dropped through the roof of the Iraqi Air Force headquarters building with devastating consequences.

Other "high tech" weaponry also came into its own, with the US Navy's BGM-109 Tomahawk cruise missile being particularly useful against targets in and around Baghdad. Reports stated that roughly 100 Tomahawks were fired by US Navy vessels including the battleships USS *Missouri* and USS *Wisconsin* in the first 24 hours but that figure is almost certainly exaggerated. What cannot be denied is the fact that many of these missiles succeeded in finding their objectives, with the BBC reporter John Simpson mentioning a bizarre episode in which a Tomahawk flew past his hotel room at a height of about 50-75 feet, following the path of the street outside.

Operations were also directed towards eliminating the threat posed by the Iraqi Air Force. While it was clearly preferable to achieve this objective by rendering the bases unusable, Allied fighter pilots were no less keen to knock Iraqi fighters down in air combat, as was proved by Captain Steve Tate of the USAF's 1st TFW who destroyed a Mirage F-1EQ with an AIM-7 Sparrow radar missile during the night.

Such encounters were rare and the job of rendering the Iraqi Air Force *hors de combat* fell mainly to strike aircraft like the British and Saudi Tornados which used the JP233 airfield denial weapon in highly dangerous low level attacks on a number of well defended air bases. Other Tornados - armed with 1,000 lb bombs - perhaps had a marginally easier time of it, using 'loft' delivery techniques to lob their ordnance on to runways but they were by no means alone in attacking the air bases, with USAF F-15E Strike Eagles and F-111F 'Aardvarks' and US Navy carrier-borne attack aircraft like the A-6E Intruder all playing a part in the aerial 'blitz'.

As day broke, there was no diminution in the allied effort but the list of targets was expanded, with British and French Jaguars operating against objectives in occupied Kuwait. All four RAF pilots that took part in an attack on a barracks came home safely but the French met stiffer resistance at Ahmed Al Jaber air base. Four of the dozen aircraft in action sustained damage from AAA and missiles, with one pilot receiving a scalp injury from a fragment of shrapnel. He was able to make it back to base but his wound did require treatment while he was still in the cockpit.

Arabian desert will be a cemetery for the invaders

In a savage editorial the Iraqi Ba'ath party newspaper *al-Thwara* painted a terrifying picture of what would happen if anyone attacked Iraq. In a statement pointed towards King Fahd of Saudi Arabia, the newspaper announced that "when the battle starts, the Arabian Desert would turn into a cemetery for the attacking invaders... the brave Iraqi Army (is) arrayed on the battlefield, has completed its preparations and is eager to fight this battle, opening the way to realizing the greater aims of the Arabs and Muslims".

Day 2

Thursday 17 January

Correspondents in Baghdad report intensified bombing of the city. A CNN correspondent says bombs are being dropped near a refinery near Baghdad.

In the first official reaction from Baghdad, Iraqi Radio says the Americans and their allies will be taught a lesson. Until now the radio has been broadcasting the Iraqi national anthem and readings from the Koran. Iraqi Radio broadcasts a message from Saddam Hussein saying "the mother of all battles" has begun.

The PLO releases a statement describing the military action as "a black day in the history of the world". The statement calls on all Arabs, Muslims and citizens of third world countries to confront the "bare-faced treachery".

The French Defence Minister, Jean-Pierre Chevenement, announces that 12 Jaguar fighterbombers have attacked targets in Kuwait.

In the first action on the ground since the outbreak of hostilities a Saudi Arabian oil refinery near the Kuwait border comes under artillery fire from inside Iraq. US aircraft and helicopters retaliate.

An Iraqi military command statement says 14 enemy aircraft have been shot down. Returning US pilots says they did not encounter any resistance from Iraqi airmen.

Saddam's Scuds hit Israel and Saudi Arabia: "We will retaliate" says Israel

Intent on drawing Israel into the war Saddam Hussein ordered his Scud ballistic missiles to be fired at Israel. So far the Israelis have not retaliated but seem very likely to should they be attacked again.

Early reports indicated that chemical war heads were used but this was later denied. Two Scuds fell on Tel Aviv, two in Haifa and a further four landed in un-populated areas. None of the Scuds were intercepted by the Israeli SAM batteries, fuelling speculation on the readiness of the costly Patriot system.

One of the first targets of the opening phase of the Air War was the spotting and destruction of both the fixed and mobile launchers that Saddam has in his arsenal. It

was widely known that he would try to involve Israel by lobbing missiles at them in spite of the fact that this would open up a second front. He gambled that it would bring about a split in the Arab unity against him. The gamble has so far failed and has set more firmly the Arab resolve against him. He also attacked Saudi Arabia within a few hours of attacking Israel.

Clearly the Allied War Plan of neutralizing all the Scud sites has so far failed in spite of what Allied spokespeople have said. This called for the identification and elimination of all the launchers within the first few hours of the campaign. Doing this would have prevented the very act that has now taken place.

What has worked flawlessly is the anti-missile missile system called Patriot. Developed by Raytheon in the US this multi-million dollar rocket has been deployed in both Saudi Arabia and Israel. It is thought though that the Israelis have not yet had enough training to use their missiles properly.

Used as a defensive line, the Patriot system is impressive. Some eight launchers contain four missiles each and behind them is the nerve centre of the system.

A mobile control station equipped with an antennae, pulse radar and generator, monitors the skies and detects any incoming missiles or aircraft. Once identified the battery commander will lock his radar onto the object and program the launcher with co-ordinates and fire the missile.

Once launched, the ground controller will make any course corrections alongside information received from radar in the missile's nose. As the missile closes its range it detonates its fragmentation warhead causing the incoming enemy missile to explode.

In its first firing in combat the system worked perfectly.

President Bush was outraged at the attack on Israel said Marlin Fitzwater and Israel's Washington Ambassador, Zalman Shuval repeated his country's right to hit back.

In a diplomatic flurry at the attack Secretary of State James Baker assured the Israeli Prime Minister that the Allies had stepped up their efforts to eliminate the Iraqi missile threat.

He appealed for restraint as both Defence Chief Shomron and Foreign Minister Levy repeat that the Iraqi attack requires a response. "It is Israel's right and duty to take steps for its defence."

THE PATRIOT STORY

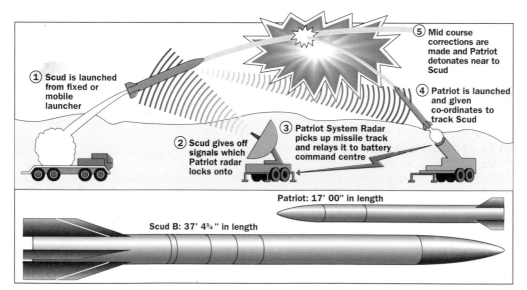

① Scud is launched from fixed or mobile launcher

② Scud gives off signals which Patriot radar locks onto

③ Patriot System Radar picks up missile track and relays it to battery command centre

④ Patriot is launched and given co-ordinates to track Scud

⑤ Mid course corrections are made and Patriot detonates near to Scud

Patriot: 17' 00" in length

Scud B: 37' 4¾" in length

The Patriot missile which destroyed the Iraqi Scud aimed at Dhahran is one of the world's most sophisticated pieces of missile technology. In its first encounter with a Scud B, it passed its test with flying colours, homing in and destroying the threat in a matter of minutes. The Patriot costs over $800,000 per missile. A salutary lesson in the cost of survival, but as Mark Harvey of the United Service Institute for Strategic Studies pointed out, "it is more a political weapon than a military one". Whether true or not, Saddam has some 108 Scud launchers available to him.

A British Tornado F3 is readied for its next mission in the around the clock air campaign. The Tornado is seeing some of the hottest action of the war .

Air operation goes on without a hitch

The air attacks continued without pause for the second day running as Iraq reeled under the relentless bombardment of its military targets.

In his now daily Press briefing, Lt-General Norman Schwarzkopf said that they had located 11 Scud launchers in Iraq and destroyed six of them. The Allies were flying over 2,000 sorties a day with a success rate of 80 per cent.

In his press briefing in London, Tom King stated that the previous night's air raids had caused significant damage to Iraq's command and control centres. Only strategic and military targets were being hit, he said, and he praised the accuracy of the bombing.

In Riyadh a US Military spokesman admitted that there had been losses of both aircraft and personnel. During the first 24 hours of the offensive, three planes had been downed from "triple A Fire" which brought the allied losses to seven. Earlier in the day British sources said that it had lost a Tornado GR1 along with its crew and a Free Kuwaiti Skyhawk was also lost with its pilot.

Because of strict censorship it is difficult to piece together the full story of the air campaign so far, but fragments can be pooled and slowly a clearer picture is emerging.

The air war is being waged primarily by the USAF, the US Navy and the RAF, alongside elements of the Royal Saudi Air Force and the Free Kuwaiti Air Force. The Italians have flown their Tornado IDSs but the one aircraft to reach its target was later shot down. French Jaguars have not gone into Iraqi air space. The Canadian squadrons are in a similar position.

DAY 3

Friday 18 January

The Soviet Foreign Minister, Alexander Bessmertnykh, says the presidential palace in Baghdad was totally destroyed during yesterday's allied air attack. Mr Bessmertnykh says intelligence reports indicate two Baghdad airports were put out of action and a number of industrial plants damaged.

President Rafsanjani says Iran will intervene in the Gulf war if its interests are threatened. He says Iran is making intensive diplomatic efforts to end the war speedily.

Crown Prince Hassan of Jordan says up to 750,000 refugees from Iraq have begun trekking towards the Jordanian border on foot. He says Jordan can only accommodate 50,000 at a time.

A correspondent for the American CNN network says all their reports are being censored.

The Italian government announces that one of its Tornado aircraft has failed to return.

The Speaker of the Iraqi Parliament, Sadi Mahdi Salih, says guns and other weapons have been handed out to the population of Baghdad so that they can join in the conflict.

Iraq's ambassador to Japan, Rashid al-Rifai, warns that Iraq reserves the right to use chemical weapons.

THE EAGLE HAS LANDED !

The McDonnell Douglas F-15 Eagle, one of the first aircraft to reach Saudi Arabia when *Desert Shield* got under way in earnest, was also one of the successes of the ensuing *Desert Storm*.

Two versions were in combat - the F-15C air superiority fighter and the F-I5E Strike Eagle.

The F-15C, employed by both the Royal Saudi Air Force and the USAF, was initially tasked with protecting Saudi airspace, operating alongside RAF Tornado F.3s in maintaining combat air patrols to counter possible threats by the Iraqi Air Force.

Once battle was joined, the F-15C also took on the fighter escort role, providing cover for strike aircraft as they flew in to bomb Iraq, and it was during one such mission that Captain Steve Tate of the USAF's 1st Tactical Fighter Wing scored the first kill of the war, when he used an AIM-7 Sparrow to destroy an Iraqi Mirage F.I on 17 January. Later, Saudi F-15C pilots also claimed a number of Iraqi victims.

Making its combat debut, the F-15E was used in the strike role. Although it was used against a variety of targets, perhaps its greatest value was in the "Scud-busting" task. In this, heavily-armed F-15Es loitered at altitude as they waited for indications of missile launch, before pressing home their attacks against the highly elusive mobile sites. Despite their best efforts, the "Scud" threat was never entirely eliminated and these and other tactical operations resulted in two F-15Es being lost in battle.

Day 4

Saturday 19 January

A further Scud missile attack on Israel is made. Israel Radio says Tel Aviv is hit and ten people are slightly wounded. US Defense Department officials say three missiles were launched. Baghdad Radio says 11 missiles were launched at Tel Aviv and Jerusalem - although there is no evidence that Jerusalem was hit.

Iraq's ambassador to Paris, Abdul Razzak al-Hashimi, says that there have been high civilian casualties and damage to civilian property after the allied air attacks on Baghdad last night.

An American military spokesman reports a clash with Iraqi forces operating from 9 Kuwaiti oil platforms in the northern Gulf. He says the forces were neutralized and 12 Iraqi prisoners were taken. They are the first Iraqis to be taken prisoner during the war.

Reuters quotes an unidentified senior US spokesman as saying President Bush has been assured by the Israelis that they will not retaliate against Scud missile attacks.

Israel announces it is in a state of war.

In Washington, the Chairman of the US Joint Chiefs of Staff, General Colin Powell, says the initial strategy for disabling Iraqi airfields and air defences has been achieved. The emphasis now is on changing towards increased attacks on concentrations of Republican Guards and other Iraqi troops.

Allied airmen paraded: Western nations appalled by Iraqi TV show

4: Yes. I would like to tell my mother

It was a shocking and disgusting sight. Seven captive Allied airmen - PoWs by any other name - were paraded on Iraqi television in a flaunting of the Geneva Convention.

One after the other, all seven spoke in stilted phrases, seeming to read from cue cards or prompters, each giving the impression that they were mentally fatigued. But it was their physical appearance that gave rise to the most immediate concern.

All the men looked battered and bruised. This could have been from the way in which they ejected from their aircraft. Cannoning out of a near super-sonic plane at any level is bound to lead to some physical battering, and a look of fatigue. But those voices... They left a haunting impression on everyone who heard or saw them on the news bulletins around the globe.

"I think our leaders and our people have wrongly attacked the peaceful people of Iraq", said US Navy Lieutenant Jeffrey Zaun (*pictured above*). His face was swollen and splattered with blood.

Another pilot, British Flight Lieutenant John Peters, could not even raise his head. He was puffy-eyed with a down-turned mouth. Signs, according to medical practitioners who saw the tapes, that the prisoners could have been maltreated.

Why did Saddam Hussein do this? What did he hope to gain from this horror show? Some would argue that Saddam was trying to show that the Allies were not invincible and could still be brought to heel. Perhaps he was trying to turn western opinion against the war. Whatever his motives, he has not succeeded, because people saw this as a total violation of the codes of the 1949 Geneva Convention. Article 17 states that "no physical or mental torture, nor any other form of coercion, may be inflicted on a prisoner of war".

Casualties claimed to total 180

In spite of the intensity of the air war and the destructive force of the constant bombing it is said that the war has claimed no more than 180 lives so far. The Allied military spokesmen are particularly reticent over casualty figures; 1 American airman killed and 18 others are missing with 22 Allied soldiers killed or missing against Iraq's claim that 94 Iraqis have been killed and 246 wounded.

The Allied military briefers say that they have no idea how many Iraqis have died in the aerial bombardment from the 7,000 sorties flown so far.

GP bombs are readied and primed before being dumped on Iraqi troop positions.

Acceptance of a long campaign

In a telephone call with the White House, Prime Minister John Major and President Bush agreed that although the war was going well the air bombardment would go on for some considerable time to come. Commanders were saying it could be months rather than weeks.

No retaliation from the military, pledges Israel

The United States was told yesterday that Israel would not retaliate over the latest Scud missile attack by Iraq.

The second attack by Saddam Hussein's mobile Scuds came prior to the daily press conference given by the Allies in Saudi Arabia. At the US briefing in Riyadh General Schwarzkopf emphasized that they were hunting down the launch sites and destroying them as fast as they could be identified.

The Israeli comment was clearly a relief for the Allies. They had been expecting a harsh reaction from Israel after a number of comments from senior politicians in Israel saying that retaliation was "almost inevitable".

In an attempt to calm the situation in Israel the US has offered to send two more Patriot batteries.

Day 5

Sunday 20 January

The US says several Americans have gone missing since the fighting started but has no knowledge of any being captured.

The correspondent in Baghdad for the American TV network CNN, Peter Arnett, says he has been told by Foreign Ministry officials that because of CNN's impartial reporting of events he and two colleagues can stay in the city.

The Ministry of Defence in Britain confirms that a third British Tornado fighter bomber has been lost.

The Allies say the number of their aircraft shot down has reached fifteen, with three more American planes lost today.

President Mitterrand says that if necessary France will attack Iraq. He says he thinks the war will last weeks rather than months. He insists the aim is to liberate Kuwait not to target Saddam Hussein.
He denies suggestions by the Defence Minister, Jean-Pierre Chevenement, that France intends only to fight in Kuwait. Mr Mitterrand says Israel realizes that to retaliate against Iraq would be to fall into a trap laid by Saddam Hussein.

In Germany anti-war demonstrators storm an army barracks in Berlin.

In Belgium demonstrations are held in Brussels calling for an end to military support for the coalition.

Given the go-ahead at last a French Jaguar streaks skyward from Dhahran Air Base. Although actively involved from the first day of the war on bombing targets inside Kuwait, it is only now that the squadrons can fly missions into Iraq itself.

TORNADO STRIKES

RAF Tornado GR1 interdictors were committed to action in the very first waves of aircraft in the early hours of Day One and remained in combat up to the end of offensive operations on 28 February. During those six weeks, well over 1,000 sorties were logged by a force that never exceeded four dozen aircraft.

Between them, they inflicted awesome damage but not achieved without cost. Six aircraft were lost, with five reported missing during the first week. Of the 12 crewmen involved, seven survived the ordeals of ejection and captivity - the remaining five were less fortunate.

In the initial stage, the Tornado was tasked with some of the most dangerous missions of the war, hitting airfields far behind Iraqi lines. One of the principal weapons used was the L2 Mk 1 - better known as the JP233 - airfield denial system. This is a bulky device, with each of the two pods carried by Tornado weighing some 5,158 lbs. Between them, they can deliver a massive quantity of sub-munitions in seconds. Those munitions include 60 SG 357 cratering bombs able to punch holes in runways, taxiways and apron areas. At the same time, 430 HB 876 mines are disgorged and these complicate the task of repair work, for some are delayed action devices while others are triggered by disturbances.

One drawback of this weapon is that the aircraft must fly low and straight while the sub-munitions are released and this makes them vulnerable to ground fire.

Day 6

Monday 21 January

In a BBC interview, Iraq's ambassador to Paris, Abdul Razzak al-Hashimi says his country will only honour the Geneva Convention in the case of those prisoners of war which the Allies admit have been captured.

After the scenes of the captured Allied airmen are shown in the West, British Defence Secretary, Tom King, says he suspects that torture and coercion has been used to obtain their statements.

At the start of a Commons debate on the Gulf, British Prime Minister, John Major, repeats his warning that securing an Iraqi withdrawal from Kuwait will not be quick. At the end of the debate parliament overwhelmingly endorses the role of British forces by 563 votes to 34.

President Bush says the Iraqi plan to hold captured Allied airmen at strategic sites will make no difference to the prosecution of the war, and that Saddam Hussein will be held accountable for the fate of the prisoners.

In Istanbul several bombs explode at a NATO building. The left-wing organization Dev Sol says it was responsible.

German Chancellor Helmut Kohl calls for a Marshall Plan-type economic aid programme for the Middle East once the Gulf war is over.

Governments' fury at Saddam's threat of PoW "human shield"

Western governments reacted angrily to the hint from the Iraqi government that PoWs would be used as "human shields". It was yet another breaking of the Geneva Convention by Iraq, which was denounced by the civilized world after the showing on TV of seven combat pilots, and their apparent denouncement of the West in waging war against Iraq

The Iraqi ambassadors in both Paris and London said that their country would have no intention of abiding by the conventions of humane treatment that the Geneva Convention laid down. In Washington President Bush promised to hold Saddam Hussein accountable.

In London, British Prime Minister John Major remarked that Iraqi forces would be held responsible after the war had ended for the way in which they were treating prisoners.

In the House of Commons Debate, the first after the war had started, he commented that, "such broadcasts are wholly objectionable in every respect. Today, there has been a reported threat to use captured airmen as human shields. Such action would be inhuman and totally contrary to the Third Geneva Convention."

As President Bush had commented, a British government spokesman said that this accountability could extend to President Saddam himself.

With the plight of every PoW becoming apparently more and more desperate, so the feeling of patriotism, with flags and ribbons, is becoming ever more apparent.

GENEVA CONVENTION CLAUSES

ARTICLE 13... PoWs "must at all time be protected against attacks, violence or intimidation and against insults and public curiosity".

ARTICLE 17..."no physical or mental torture, nor any form of coercion, may be inflicted on prisoners of war".

Nuclear reactors not hit says Pentagon

The Pentagon has denied an earlier British report that Iraq's nuclear reactors had been hit.

Although "nuclear facilities" had been targeted, it was classified information as to which and what type the facilities were. As such, no information would be divulged. There has been concern that if the Allies attacked nuclear reactors there would be widespread radiation fallout.

Over 4,000 Iraqi military personnel have been killed according to the Kurdistan Democratic Party. This was`based on first-hand assessments and "includes only those installations we are convinced were hit" the spokesman said. "It doesn't include bombing in the south or the attacks on troop concentrations there".

Iraqi and Allied casualty figures continue to differ widely, with journalists pressing the daily briefers in Riyadh, Washington and London for more information.

While most of the action was directed towards gaining air supremacy and superiority the troops on the ground were experiencing the vagaries of the Saudi climate. Unusually heavy winter rains were turning the desert tracks into quagmires.

Saddam to be personally targeted?

The US government has decided to hold Saddam Hussein personally responsible for war crimes.

In a statement issued by the White House, spokesman Marlin Fitzwater said that he could not rule out the possibility of Allied forces undertaking a mission to capture Saddam Hussein for mistreating PoWs, but Saddam is not being considered a personal target at the present time. How he would be targeted is open to speculation.

From Day One of the war the Allies have had special forces operating inside Iraq on covert operational assignments and it can be safely assumed that, if the order was given, then one of these special teams would carry out the operation.

Iraq admits to more bomb damage

Very slowly it is now becoming apparent that Iraq is being systematically paralyzed from the air. Iraqi Radio announced that TV and power had been cut off in northern Iraq due to US bombing raids by F-111s.

What this is doing to the civilian population can only be guessed at. The psychological pressure on Iraq's Army is severe but, as yet, there are no reports of deserters.

Day 7

Tuesday 22 January

The US says it has rescued one of its pilots shot down over the Iraqi desert. Two bombers traced the pilot's SOS signal and destroyed an Iraqi truck as a helicopter arrived to pick him up.

Police in Tokyo warn that members of the Japanese Red Army terrorist group may be planning to make attacks in Europe as part of a campaign to support Iraq.

The European Community condemns what it calls Iraq's unscrupulous use of PoWs, and say their treatment could constitute a war crime.

Hundreds of refugees leaving Iraq arrive at an international Red Cross camp on the Jordanian border. They are to be sent on to their countries of origin - mainly Egypt, Sudan, India and Bangladesh. UN officials say that up to 750,000 foreigners may be waiting to leave Iraq once they feel that travel is safe enough.

The Prime Minister of the Afghan guerrilla groups' interim government, Professor Abdul Rasul Sayeef, condemns the war in the Gulf as one imposed on innocent Muslims.

In a letter to UN Secretary General Pérez de Cuéllar from Iraq's UN ambassador, Abul al-Anbari, Iraq says that 41 civilians have been killed and 191 injured in air and missile attacks.

Scud attack hits homes in Tel Aviv: Israel may finally take action

More Scud missiles have been aimed at Israel - and they have succeeded in getting through to their targets.

In the latest attack on Tel Aviv three people died and and more than 70 were injured; of that number, over 10 were children. The Scuds hit a residential district and caused more damage than the two previous attacks put together remarked an Israeli military spokesman.

It was the third attack by Iraq on Israel and the first after President Bush had ordered US troops to be deployed there. That order, issued last Sunday, was to help the Israeli Patriot crews who had not yet reached a level of experience for them to use the system proficiently enough. US crews, alongside more missile systems, were drafted in at 48 hours notice, mainly from reserve units operating with the United States Army in Europe.

In the last attack by Iraq two Patriot missiles were fired and witnesses saw the interception of one Scud. The other got through and landed with devastating results.

Apart from the physical damage and the loss of lives, the Iraqis are waging a campaign of terror on the civil population and severely testing the restraint of Israel's politicos.

So far the war heads of the Scuds have contained only conventional armaments but they do have the capacity to be used with chemicals and this factor is weighing more and more on the minds of politicians and civilians alike.

"Israel has shown remarkable restraint in the face of this aggression" said

Another Scud lands on Tel Aviv hitting a residential district. The consequences of this latest attack are fraught with danger as the Iraqis are bent on opening a second front.

President Bush. "We consult the government of Israel and will continue doing so as events unfold."

That comment was echoed in London by British Prime Minister John Major, " ...at this bitter moment we hope that they will not cast off the restraint that they have shown so far and give Saddam Hussein the satisfaction of drawing them into the conflict."   The latest act of aggression to the Israelis was hard to bear

in the Knesset. One prominent Israeli put it succinctly. "It is not a question of whether Israel will retaliate but rather when and how."

Some of the injuries that occurred during the latest attack were very serious, and in an interview on CNN the Deputy Prime Minister of Israel said, "As much as we appreciate the excellent work done by the Patriot crews, that gives only a partial answer and tonight demonstrates that."

Burning well-heads in the al-Wafra oilfield bear bleak testimony to the Pentagon's claim that it was monitoring oil field fires in Kuwait. Treated with caution by the rest of the Allies, there is now no disputing that this is happening.

Soviets say 90% of bombing missions missing targets

Interfax, the Soviet news agency said that it had learned from an unidentified Soviet Army source that 90 percent of the bombing missions undertaken by the allies were missing their targets. "A large part of the Iraqi aircraft and airports have not been hit, despite all claims to the contrary. Air bases in Iraq are very well camouflaged and extremely hard to detect."

Bad weather has been used as an excuse, the agency said.

Over 10,000 sorties had been made by the Allies so far, with the news that another British Tornado GR1 had been lost to enemy fire.

Special Forces rescued downed US pilot

It is rarely admitted that they even exist but such was the pleasure that one of their comrades had been rescued from under the very noses of the enemy, that, for once they actually let the information leak out.

After yesterday's announcement that a USAF pilot had been picked up, it has now emerged from Washington DC that his rescue was carried out by one of its Special Force Groups. Possibly a team from the 1st SOW (Special Operations Wing),originating from Hulbert Field, Florida, which has been out in the Gulf since *Desert Shield* began.

Day 8
Wednesday 23 January

The remains of what the Iraqi government says was a powder milk factory destroyed by allied bombing raids, is visited by a CNN reporter. The Americans say it was a heavily fortified installation which they believe was involved in the production of weapons for biological warfare.

Iraq's Oil Ministry announces the suspension of the sale of petrol and fuel oil at filling stations throughout the country.

Baghdad Radio reports that two Iraqi citizens have captured a British pilot whose Tornado was shot down over the south of Iraq.

The American Defense Secretary, Dick Cheney, says the first week of the Allied attempt to drive Iraq out of Kuwait has gone very well. The American Chief of Staff, General Colin Powell, acknowledges that they have faced problems with the weather and they were having to do more than they had originally planned to locate Iraq's Scud missiles. He says air superiority has been achieved. The Allied forces will now concentrate on Iraq's positions in Kuwait and on the army's food and energy stock piles.

FLOATING AIR BASES

During *Desert Storm*, no fewer than half-a-dozen US Navy aircraft carriers constituted the centrepiece of several battle groups that were operating in the Red Sea and the Gulf. Between them, these six ships mustered almost exactly 500 aircraft and helicopters. Their commitment to the Allied air offensive was a substantial and important one.

Air superiority, interdiction, close air support, electronic warfare and airborne early warning were all missions that were routinely undertaken from these floating air bases, each of which was part of an organization known as a Carrier Air Wing (CVW).

In simple terms, the CVW is responsible for directing the operations of aircraft at sea, whether they be concerned with peacetime training or wartime combat action. However, the composition of the Carrier Air Wings that embarked on these vessels did vary slightly from the norm.

Apart from one notable exception, all the large carriers - ships like the USS *Saratoga*, USS *Independence* and USS *America* - deployed with the so-called "conventional" type of CVW.

There were variations. One of these was provided by the USS *Roosevelt*, which carried the aptly-named "Roosevelt" type of CVW that will eventually become standard throughout the fleet. As with the "conventional" type of CVW, the number of aircraft embarked was 86, but F-14 and F/A-18 elements were reduced in order to accommodate an additional medium attack squadron with the A-6E.

The other variation concerned the USS *Midway*, a much smaller vessel which went into action with a CVW named after its recently retired sister ship, the USS *Coral Sea*. On the *Midway*, three F/A18 squadrons with a total of 36 aircraft shared responsibility for fighter and light attack tasks and they were supported by a pair of medium attack squadrons which operated some 16 A-6E and KA-6D Intruders between them. Other elements consisted of four EA-6Bs, four E-2Cs and six SH-3Hs, giving a fully-laden complement of 66 aircraft and helicopters.

BELOW: *An F/A-18 Hornet of VFA 125 about to launch off the deck of the USS* Midway *during the opening days of war.*

ABOVE: *An A-6 Prowler sits on deck, its wings folded awaiting its next mission over Iraqi air space.*

ABOVE: *The USS* Independence *on station during* Desert Shield. *She returned to the US in December 1990.*

Day 9

Thursday 24 January

British Defence Secretary Tom King announces the loss in action of Britain's fifth Tornado aircraft. He announces that Buccaneer aircraft with advanced laser equipment are being sent to the Gulf with two more army regiments which will be used in a support role.

A British military spokesman in Saudi Arabia says the Royal Navy is engaged in offensive operations in the Gulf for the first time, when a Lynx helicopter operating from HMS *Cardiff* spots three Iraqi vessels. During the operation that follows, two minesweepers are sunk, and the occupied Kuwaiti island of Qaruh from which they operate is recaptured, the first Kuwaiti territory to be liberated. Three Iraqis are killed in the operation and 51 captured.

The Americans say one of their F-16s was shot down by ground fire over Kuwait. They say the pilot managed to ditch the aircraft in the Gulf and was rescued by helicopter.

The Director of the US FBI, Judge William Sessions, says international terrorists are operating in the United States.

British Prime Minister, John Major, says that the land battle in the Gulf will not be fought until Iraqi land forces have been weakened, in order to minimize casualties.

"Environmental terrorism" - Pentagon

The Pentagon summed it up briefly and well. It was "environmental terrorism".

Following on from the exploding of the oil wells the Iraqis have now turned their attention to the Gulf itself. Not satisfied with polluting the atmosphere, they are now pumping oil out into the sea and causing an oil slick that will be tens of times bigger than the one caused by the *Exxon Valdez* in Alaska.

There are strategic reasons, the US military say, for this but nothing that they "cannot get around". An amphibious landing has always looked a very likely bet, but a slick would not stop an amphibious assault, even though wading through crude oil and getting it clogged up in machinery as troops and vehicles came ashore, would be bound to hinder any assault.

If Saddam Hussein set the oil on fire then the problems would be made much more difficult - crude oil, however, does not burn easily and with the allies having total air superiority they would be able to forestall any serious attempts by the Iraqis. In fact there was really no rational reason for doing what Saddam did. President Bush declared: "It looks desperate. It looks last gasp... It looks kind of sick."

The oil slick is reported to be over 20 miles wide and growing fast. It is coming from the Sea Island Terminal from which tankers load offshore. Two further sites of spillage have been identified, and these are from oil tankers which are berthed at the Kuwaiti occupied port of Mina al-Ahamadi. Millions of gallons have been pouring into the sea and there is no respite say intelligence sources who have been monitoring the slick for two days on satellite photographs.

With the prevailing winds and currents in the Northern Gulf, it will not be long before the oil threatens Saudi Arabia. island of Bahrain.

An innocent victim of the oil slick and one of the first casualties of the "eco-war".

MIRAGE KILLER

The news was first broken a few hours into the previous day but the euphoria is still resonant on the Dhahran ramp as a young Royal Saudi Air Force pilot claimed two kills from his F-15 Eagle. It was the first Saudi kills of the war, and Captain Chamrani, a veteran of seven years, was jubilant.

He was interviewed on CNN after his encounter with the two Iraqi Mirages and said that any pilot in his position would have been able to do the same thing, and any Iraqi pilot would have found it an equally hard situation to get out of.

The Royal Saudi Air force is equipped with three squadrons of 60 F-15Es and 42 F-15Cs organized into three interceptor squadrons. Besides this the RSAF can boast three squadrons of 20 British Tornados. All together a pool of 180 combat ready aircraft is available. The pilots are trained to a very high standard, passing through the best USAF and RAF flying schools.

The war hots up but air offensive may take 100,000 sorties

In spite of the apparent success of the air campaign it is still forecast to go on for at least 100,000 sorties. This means that the ground war will not begin until mid-February.

During the previous 24 hours some 2,707 missions had been flown, the largest single day total of the war so far. This brings the total number of sorties to 17,500. Allied aircraft losses are given as 25, with 27 airmen missing. Iraqi losses to date are, the Allies maintain, 41.

Iraq claims that it has shot down over 200 planes, taken 20 PoWs, has had 101 civilians killed and 90 soldiers. The Kurds put the total number of soldiers killed at 10,000.

Other indicators from Iraq give the impression that all is not well. There are unconfirmed reports that Saddam Hussein has had his top air force commanders shot. They have been blamed for the ineffectiveness of the war and "the destruction of 26 out of Iraq's 100 Scud missiles and 300 aircraft out of 700".

At sea the capture yesterday of the tiny island of Qaruh was a turning point in the maritime war. The liberation has given a massive psychological boost to the Kuwaitis in occupied Kuwait as well as to Kuwaiti resistance fighters.

It was a fierce fight, with the Royal Navy and US Navy taking part. Five hours of bombing and strafing by US aircraft as well as RN assault helicopters resulted in the capture of the island and 51 prisoners.

Day 10

Friday 25 January

Iraqi Air Force planes begin to arrive in Iran. The Iranians say seven have arrived. The Pentagon says that at least 12 fighters, including Mirage F-1 aircraft, and 12 transport planes arrive during the day. Iran says that aircraft landing on its territory from either side will be held until the conflict ends.

The Australian Defence Department announces that the country is sending a team of divers to the Gulf to disarm mines.

A German government spokesman announces a package of aid worth $1,200 million (US dollars) to Egypt, Jordan, Turkey and Israel.

Israel comes under further attack from Scud missiles. Army spokesman General Nachman Shai says seven missiles were hit or damaged by Patriot anti-missile rockets. One person is reported killed and several injured in the attack. Baghdad Radio says three missiles were fired at Tel Aviv and one at Haifa.

The Chief of Staff of the French armed forces, General Maurice Schmitt, says the Allies have achieved total control of the skies over Iraq.

A CNN reporter is taken by Iraqi officials to the town of Al-Dour, where he counts 20 destroyed homes, and is told 24 civilians have been killed.

THE BONFIRES OF HELL

After two days of monitoring by surveillance aircraft, it seemed clear that Saddam Hussein had at last started what the world dreaded - ecological warfare. When the first reports came through from the Pentagon, the British and other allies were cautious of interpreting too much from the photographs but all now seems to be true. The Iraqi Army is systematically destroying each and every well-head in the al-Wafra oilfield and there is no reason to suppose that they will not continue until all the well-heads in Kuwait are alight. It is a terrible revenge on a country so small and so dependent on oil.

The ecological damage is incalculable. How far into the atmosphere will the smoke go and what will the long-term effects be? How many people will be affected and what about the region's wildlife?

Day 11

Saturday 26 January

A military spokesman says that the oil spill in the Gulf is getting larger and is now moving south at a rate of 20 miles per day. It is causing a great deal of damage to both bird and marine life and is likely to threaten the salt-water purification plants of Saudi Arabia.

Anti-war demonstrators converge on Bonn in the biggest protest so far in Germany. Demonstrations are also held in London, Washington DC, Los Angeles and San Francisco.

A decree, published by Iraq's Revolutionary Council, says that anyone who is killed in the course of "Fedayeen action" against the forces confronting Iraq will be officially designated "Martyr of the Mother of Battles".

A CNN reporter is shown destruction in civilian areas of the town of Najaf.

Jordan requests Iraq to open its border to allow an estimated 5,000 refugees to leave.

US Secretary of State, James Baker, announces that Saudi Arabia has pledged a further $13,500 million (US dollars) towards US war costs.

On German TV, Turkish President Ozal says his country would respond to any Iraqi attack.

Smart bomb scores direct hit to stem oil flow

It has been revealed today that the USAF performed a "surgical strike" last Saturday, 26 January and bombed oil pressure controls of the Sea Island off-shore terminal.

The bombing, using F-111 aircraft, was a success, said General Schwarzkopf today, as the flow of oil into the sea was diminishing. "It was certainly a success because we achieved what we intended to" ,he said.

The raid had occurred at 10.30 pm (local time) and the F-111s used GBU-15 bombs which use TV or infra-red to home onto their target.

Saudi officials are even now floating out booms to protect vital desalination plants that could easily become affected by the oil slick as it continues to drift down the coast. The slick is slowly breaking up into a number of smaller ones, but there is still 13 miles of oil in the pipes even if the oil has since been stemmed.

The environmental tragedy is easy to comprehend as birds and sea animals are washed ashore, either dead or so covered in oil that they might as well be. Experts hoping to be able to rescue the animals are being held up trying to get into Saudi Arabia because it is a war zone.

An F-111 streaks away from a bomb-run. It was one of these aircraft that delivered, with pin-point accuracy, the bombs which cut off the oil flow.

CASUALTIES AND LOSSES

	IRAQI FIGURES	ALLIED FIGURES
Military		
dead	90	1
missing or captured	0	27
Civilians		
dead	125	8
missing or captured	136	42
Aircraft losses	200	24
Shipping losses	-	18
Israel		
dead		4
Civilian casualties		128

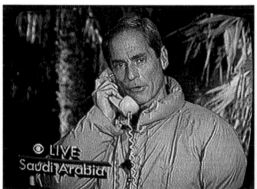

Concern grows for CBS team

There is still no news of the whereabouts of the Columbia Broadcasting System news crew, which includes veteran reporter Bob Simon (*see above*), that went missing on 24 January when their empty car was found near the Kuwaiti border.

The Navies of both US and Britain are continuing to patrol with increasing vigour as they move slowly up the northern Gulf. Contact with enemy patrol boats is increasing and there are reports of imminent US Marine exercises just south of Kuwait.

Land forces mass near border

It is cold and damp. Rain has been falling in massive amounts and the desert is a morass of mud and vehicles.

In spite of this the Allied army is on the move. After the limelight being grabbed by the air crews, it is now time for the ground forces to step up a notch and move their forces into staging areas in preparation for the ground assault that now seems inevitable. As well as a general re-positioning of forces, the artillery are shelling enemy positions, softening them up and adding their weight to the already massive attention that the Iraqis are getting from the air.

Each and every member of the Allied forces knows that it cannot be long before the troops are ordered in.

Day 12
Sunday 27 January

The Iranian Red Crescent Society announces a donation of food to the people of Iraq.

The British Defence Secretary, Tom King, says in a BBC interview that the aims of US resolutions would not be achieved if Iraq forces merely withdrew to Iraq's border with Kuwait, so they could repeat the invasion.

Jordanian officials say that thousands of refugees trying to reach Jordan from Iraq have been ordered back to Baghdad for exit visas.

The Iranian News Agency reports that rain polluted with oil has fallen on Iran today.

A US Navy spokesman says a group of 20 to 30 Iraqi soldiers stranded on the island of Um al-Maradim have indicated their wish to surrender.

General Norman Schwarzkopf says 39 Iraqi aircraft have now flown to Iran, including some of its best fighters.

A letter from Iraqi Foreign Minister Tariq Aziz to Javier Pérez de Cuéllar, is broadcast by Baghdad Radio. The letter says Iraq holds the UN Secretary General personally responsible for the continuing attacks on its territory.

US military spokesman, Major George Cutchall, says Iraqi troops have planted an estimated 500,000 mines inside Kuwait.

100 Iraqi planes now in Iran. Defection mystery deepens

Over 100 aircraft, at least 39 of which are combat types, have now flown over the border into northern Iran, well away from the bombing sorties of the allied air forces.

It had been assumed both in Washington and London that this moving of air assets was a series of deliberate defections on the part of the Iraqi military. Now no one is too sure. It looks increasingly like a deliberate policy. Ensuring that the best aircraft are saved and can live to fight another day.

"This is good news", said Tom King, the British Defence Secretary. It means that they are out of the fight.

The US has said that it was satisfied with what Iran gave as reassurances that the Iraqi planes that had been flown to Iran would not be used and would remain

RULING THE SKIES

Of late, much has been said about the terms "air superiority" and "air supremacy". How is it defined? "Air superiority" is the ability for an air power to use any aircraft it likes, when it likes, unhindered by enemy aircraft. "Air supremacy", a phrase never used by the US, means denying the enemy the chance of mounting a threat because he cannot get airborne or does not have enough aircraft to do it.

The Navy is on constant alert and ever mindful that the Iraqis may launch a missile attack with Exocets or even chemicals. This sailor in full chemical clothing primes a close support weapon in the northern Gulf.

there until the end of the war. The Pentagon claimed that more than 80 were in neutral Iran but they would not be drawn on whether they were defections or not.

Among the aircraft known to be in Iraq are whole squadrons of Mig-29 Fulcrums and Mirage F-1s, backed up by support aircraft, including Soviet Ilyushin-76 transports and two out of Iraq's three AWAC (Airborne Warning and Control) aircraft.

At the start of the war it was known that Saddam Hussein had over 700 aircraft at his disposal. Prior to the start of hostilities they were dispersed to the hundreds of airfields that he has scattered around the country. Many were built with hardened shelters which are notoriously hard to bomb and seriously damage and which have been the subject of sustained aerial attacks using new bombing techniques and high explosive bombs of 1,000 or 2,000 lbs to crack open the shelters.

Airlift under way to combat oil pollution

The British Government took positive steps in combating the ever growing oil slick that continues to threaten the mid and southern Gulf by ordering an emergency airlift of anti-pollution equipment. Even though the bombing mission that took place last Saturday appears to have been successful, the oil slick continues to grow.

Iraq accused the Allies of "igniting a fire and [that] led to a flow of quantities of oil to the waters of the Gulf". US bombing of tankers moored in the Gulf caused the spillage, said Iraq. Not so, said the US.

These Saudis view the on-coming oil slick with great concern. If it was a military ploy by Iraq to forestall an amphibious assault then the secondary pay-off will be the massive problems which will be caused by the slick fouling the fresh-water plants of Saudi Arabia.

Buccaneers join the battle

The ancient (in aviation terms), and venerated Buccaneer has joined its fellow aircraft in the Gulf. Called up last week it was announced that "half a squadron of these ageing airframes would be leaving Scotland for the Gulf as soon as they could".

Speculation was briefly rife, but as soon as the news of the change in Tornado bombing tactics was announced it became clear what role these aircraft would play.

In spite of their age they have some of the most up-to-date avionics packages bolted into them. Among them is a guidance system which can help the Tornado GR1 and Jaguar pilots use their weapons more accurately.

With the Buccaneers flying at a higher altitude than the other plane and sending a laser beam down onto the target, the bomb-carrying plane can then drop its ordnance which "rides" down the beam to detonate with its target.

Day 13
Monday 28 January

US Secretary of Defense, Dick Cheney, says there is no need to rush into a land assault that would mean unnecessary casualties. He says US forces will be ready to launch a ground offensive by the end of February.

In a letter to the Director of the World Health Association, the Iraqi Health Minister calls on the organization to "take a more serious position" on the environmental threat arising from the foreign military presence in the region - especially the deployment of nuclear warheads.

At the beginning of a three -day debate in the Japanese parliament, the leader of the opposition Socialist Party, Takako Doi, says the proposal to provide $9,000 million (US dollars) in aid to the Allied war effort is a breach of the country's constitution.

The UN Disaster Relief Organization says nine hundred, mostly Jordanian, refugees have been allowed to cross the border from Iraq into Jordan.

President Bush says that the US does not seek the destruction or destabilization of Iraq and reaffirms that the US forces will leave the Gulf region as soon as their mission is complete.

THE COLOURS OF WAR

Camouflage is a highly important aspect of warfare and one which is now taken very seriously indeed.

Perhaps the most noticeable camouflage scheme was seen in the air and was sported by a number of British aircraft who went "pink" almost overnight. This experimental colour scheme had been worked on and proven in the late sixties but is only now being put to the operational test.

Whilst USAF aircraft were instantly deployed and flown over from the US without time or need to re-paint them, British Jaguars were receiving an instant coat of desert camouflage paint. Later this was extended to other aircraft like the Tornado and helicopters.

The US Navy had recently adopted a new scheme which to all but the very knowledgeable was the same as the old one. The one variation that can be seen and enjoyed though is a return to the flamboyant tail markings on one aircraft in every squadron - usually this turns out to be the commander's mount.

Many other "grey" aircraft could be seen, including Canadian CF-18A Hornets and US Marine F-18s. The Marines had a number of operational schemes, and grey, green and sand-coloured helicopters could often be seen mixing with US Army Olive.

BELOW:*A CF-18 Hornet of 409 "Nighthawk" Squadron deployed into the Gulf from Baden-Sollingen in Germany.*

BELOW: *The US Navy scheme flown by VFA-131 from CVW 7 embarked on USS* Dwight D Eisenhower *during* Desert Shield.

ABOVE: *The underside view of the CAF aircraft showing the last three digits of the serial for the individual aircraft letter code number.*

ABOVE: *The scheme used on the upper side of USN VFA-131 aircraft. Note the small "star and bar" on the wing and a Modex number on the flap to assist deck operations.*

BELOW: *An RAF Hercules C Mk1 which was the first aircraft to have the experimental colour scheme given to it during trials in 1968.*

BELOW: *A "pink" Jaguar GR1A, which was one of the first aircraft to arrive in the Gulf during August 1990.*

ABOVE: *A Royal Saudi Air Force Tornado IDS from No 70 Squadron, showing the hard edged desert camouflage favoured by the Saudis. This scheme was first applied to RSAF aircraft in the* late 1980s and has been adapted for use on other aircraft like the BA Hawk. The F-15 colour scheme continues to be grey and follows the basic colour scheme of other USAF based F-15s.

Day 14

Tuesday 29 January

A statement broadcast by Iraqi Radio says that a captured pilot from the Allied force was killed last night in an air attack on the Ministry of Industry building in Baghdad.

The UN says a group of 30 refugees has crossed into Syria from Iraq - the first since the Gulf conflict started.

White House spokesman, Marlin Fitzwater, says the US remains concerned about the continuing exodus of Iraqi planes to Iran, although it has received assurances through a third party that Iran would keep its word and impound them until the war ends.

A US military official describes an overnight infiltration in northern Saudi Arabia. He says Saudi border guards were ambushed by a dozen Iraqi soldiers who crossed two kilometers over the border. Three Saudis were wounded and the Iraqis accidentally killed their own officer in an exchange of fire.

British military spokesmen say that a British, US and Saudi attack was made on a group of 17 Iraqi patrol vessels off the coast of the island of Maradin. Five were sunk and the remainder scattered and headed for the Kuwaiti coastline.

Marines lose "twelve" men in border clash with Iraqis

The US Commander in the Gulf, General Norman Schwarzkopf, ran a press briefing this afternoon that mixed sadness with joy.

In overnight clashes the Iraqis have been probing the border with Saudi Arabia and Kuwait. Firefights had developed and during the action 12, later modified to 11, marines were reported killed.

Some 24 Iraqi tanks were destroyed as well as 13 other vehicles in the incident, the details of which are obviously unclear. Confusion is still apparent as one member of the military contradicts another with regard to even the simplest of details of the events.

Some press reporters continue to say that the fighting is still going on and that this was not an overnight border raid as the military would have people believe but a full scale attack along a number of points on the Saudi-Kuwaiti border.

The ground forces are straining at the leash and are ready for a fight. Tanks and other armour are in staging areas, positioned just outside Iraqi artillery range. From being 40 miles from the border a few days ago they are less than 20 now.

GENERAL NORMAN SCHWARZKOPF

....

Overall Commander of the Allied forces in the Middle East. It was mainly his strategy, the encircling movement round the entire Iraqi army in the field (based upon Hannibal's defeat of the Romans at Cannae in 216 BC) that won the Allies their brisk and brilliant victory.'Stormin' Norman', as the war journalists enjoyed calling him, is 56. He served in Vietnam as an adviser to the South Vietnamese airborne division and as a battalion commander in the 23rd Infantry Division. He is considered an expert on desert warfare and had the special advantage of having recently served as deputy chief for operations and plans.

"We have air supremacy" - says Schwarzkopf

The news that General Schwarzkopf brought regarding the prosecution of the air war was much better than the few carefully chosen words that were spoken about the ground war.

"The allies now have air supremacy" he said. Giving details of the last two weeks fighting he said that he was more than happy with the way that events were progressing, but that there was still a lot more to be done, and the troops on the ground would not be set on their appointed tasks until the Iraqi Army had lost a specific percentage of men and machinery. The precision attacks against the hardened shelters were going well, with over 70 destroyed, and the Iraqis have lost control of their central command and "Iraqi aircraft are running out of places to hide".

Civilian suffering high

Reports are coming out of Iraq about the high death toll of the civilian population of Iraq. This is something that the military briefers refuse to be drawn on.

Baghdad and other large towns in the country are said to be without water and electricity. People were being maimed and killed almost hourly. The bombing raids were continuous; somewhere there was always the distant scream of a jet or the dull thud of bombs and artillery shells exploding.

Food was in short supply and meat rare, vegetables were available, but expensive and the price of bread had gone up almost 30 times. People knew that they had to get away but they did not know where to go.

Bomb damage in one of Baghdad's suburbs. The civilian population is hit hard in spite of what the military say .

Day 15

Wednesday 30 January

The admiral commanding Italy's naval contingent in the Gulf, Rear Admiral Mario Buracchia, resigns following the publication of an article in the magazine *Famiglia Christiana*. In the article the admiral says he felt the conflict could have been avoided had the Allies given sanctions a chance to work.

UN Secretary, Javier Pérez de Cuéllar, sends a reply to the letter sent by Iraqi Foreign Minister, Tariq Aziz, in which he rejects the personal attack made on him. The Secretary General renews his appeal for Iraq to withdraw from Kuwait.

British Foreign Minister, Douglas Hurd, holds talks in Bonn with German Foreign Minister Hans-Dietrich Genscher who announces that Germany will give Britain $540 million (US dollars) to help defray the costs of the Gulf war.

The OECD meeting in Paris describes Iraq's dumping of oil into the Gulf as a crime against the environment and a violation of international law.

Jordan's Foreign Minister, Taher al-Masri, says that four of its nationals and one Egyptian were killed in deliberate and brutal Allied air attacks on the Baghdad to Amman road.

Neo-Nazis in Germany say they have received more than 500 volunteers to go to the Gulf to fight for Iraq.

Ground battles erupt along border: Iraqis holding onto border town as fighting rages

needed they are calling in air support from both AV-8B Harriers, Cobra gunships and A-10 tankbusters. The fact that the Saudis and pan-Arab forces are being used in the counter attacks are, no doubt, for political reasons.

The incident began yesterday when 16 T-55 Soviet-built tanks rolled down the road and through the border crossing.

By today parts of Khafji were back in the hands of Saudi Arabia but a number of Iraqi snipers were still holed up in some of the central streets.

The sudden eruption of fighting comes amid conflicting reports that said that the Americans opened up an artillery barrage on Iraqi positions just over the Kuwaiti border on Tuesday.

These were to supplement the constant bombing missions that were going on. Other sources said that a raid had taken place and that up to 50 Iraqi tanks had driven over the border defences and were driven back only after aircraft had been called in to help. In the attack 13 enemy tanks were destroyed. Some 30 minutes later another incursion took place further east toward the coast. Little information from that incident has been forthcoming except that the enemy were in 16 APCs (armoured personnel carriers).

There was a further probing attack by the Iraqis at Ruqi near the border with Iraq, Kuwait and Saudi Arabia. It appears from the scant evidence that has come through, that an artillery duel took place and that after the skirmish the Iraqis withdrew. American armour is massing along the roads near to Ruqi and deploying on a broad front as if to tempt the Iraqis out of their defensive positions so that the Americans can bring their own fire-power to bear.

Only two weeks to the day after the "liberation of Kuwait" began, the Iraqis are on the offensive.

Late yesterday, after it was announced that 11 US marines had been killed, Iraqi ground forces continued to press forward attacks along the Kuwaiti borders for the second successive night.

The most serious incident, which continues, according to some press sources, is that the border town of al-Khafji has been taken by Iraqi troops and that, in spite of counter-attacks by Saudi and Qatari troops, they are still there.

The US Marines, who are deployed in that area, are adding their own fire-power (*see picture above*), but are keeping out of any main assault to retake the town. As

17 Iraqi patrol boats sunk in naval clash

At the same time as the Iraqis were probing the strength of the Allied land forces, the British navy was engaged in a successful attack on an Iraqi flotilla.

Some 17 landing craft were making their way under cover of darkness down the coastline of Kuwait when they were attacked by Lynx helicopters launched from British warships and armed with Sea Skua missiles. Other Allied aircraft were also called in to help in the action.

RAF Jaguars were of paramount importance to the event having pinpointed the flotilla off Mina Saud.

It is not known whether these aircraft used their new Canadian-bought CRV 7 rockets during the engagement. These are borne in by the aircrafts under wing pods and are the highest velocity rockets used by the West's air forces. Their killing power is considerable.

Four amphibious assault craft were sunk and another 12 damaged, however there is no estimate of how many troops they were carrying or how many drowned.

During the last two days the Navy has been in constant action in the Gulf with seven ships sunk by the Allies.

This means that over one third of Iraq's navy, small though it is, has been crippled or sunk.

A continuing fear among the crewmen of all the Allied vessels is the fear of Exocet attack. This threat is posed from both sea and air. The British in particular, after the Falklands experience with Argentine Exocet attacks, will be keen to smash as much of, if not all Iraq's navy so that the threat is as limited as possible.

When the Saudi Air Force downed the two Iraqi Mirages last week it was safely assumed that this was a potential attack on the Allied ships in the Northern Gulf.

A tranquil scene aboard HMS London *as her Lynx helicopter flies back in after "point duty". A few hours later she was again airborne heading south for the engagement with the assault flotilla near Mina Saud.*

Day 16

Thursday 31 January

In an interview with the London *Times*, British Prime Minister, John Major, says he cannot rule out military action against Iraq after their forces have left Kuwait. He says that a Western naval and air presence including British participation is likely in the region, after the war ends.

The UN Environment Programme says it is sending a team to investigate the oil slick in the Gulf, and calls a special meeting in Geneva to prepare an international strategy to deal with the contamination.

British Defence Secretary, Tom King, says he believes it is very likely that Iraq will use chemical weapons. He also tells Parliament that the government has agreed to a US request to station B-52 bombers at RAF Fairford in Gloucestershire from where bombing raids will be mounted on Iraqi targets.

The French Foreign Ministry confirms that senior official François Scheer is in Tehran, but will not be meeting any members of an Iraqi delegation headed by deputy Prime Minister Saadoun Hammadi which has just arrived.

US Vice-President Dan Quayle visits Britain. He arrives at RAF Lakenheath where he is welcomed by US Forces personnel. He later holds talks with Prime Minister John Major.

Iraqi armour on the move: 60,000 troops heading for border?

Iraqi troops are still in al-Khafji tonight refusing to be flushed out even though they are cut off and no retreat is now possible. The main town was retaken about mid-day today after 36 hours of bitter fighting.

The main parts of Khafji are controlled by the Allies after Saudi National Guard and elements of the Qatar Army, supported by troops from the US Marines 1st Division, retook the town. The pockets of sniper resistance are small but irritating.

What seems to be more worrying is the apparent build-up of Iraqi troops "roughly 800 to 1,000 vehicles... moving...in small groups, in convoys. There is no sign of the Iraqis retreating; vehicles are still heading south".

"It's almost like you flipped on the light in the kitchen at night and cockroaches started scurrying, and we're killing them." USAF Colonel Dick White was quoted as saying. "It's exactly what we're looking for." US Marine Corps pilots were equally

descriptive about the movements that they had seen on the roads. All activity was pointing to a push south. Was Khafji the start of a broader move? Perhaps a feinting move on the part of the Iraqis.

If this troop movement is true, then the A-10s will have a field-day - a "turkey shoot", to quote one Warthog pilot. With General Schwarzkopf pointing to Allied air supremacy and not a single challenge of late from the Iraqi Air Force the movement south seems bizarre, and totally contradictory to the strategy of war.

"Based on what we have seen", said Brigadier-General Pat Stevens at a Pentagon briefing, "he may be looking for some sort of victory...some sort of action from which he can gain confidence."

Commenting on the Khafji battle Brig-General Stevens said over 350 aircraft had been used against Iraqi forces in the Khafji area.

It was Prime Minister John Major, in London, who added a little more news - that house-to-house searches were being carried out in Khafji to ensure that the town would be cleared of Iraqi forces. Urban warfare is hard and bitter and presaged the fact that this is what it could be like taking Kuwait City should the Iraqis decide on a strategic withdrawal.

With most of the Iraqi troops gone in the town, some fighting was still going on to the north near the Kuwaiti border. So far over 160 prisoners have been taken.

An official Saudi spokesman proudly announced that "the battle has ended with the forces of Saudi Arabia victorious."

Baghdad Radio pointed out that Saddam Hussein himself commanded the battle for Khafji from Kuwait; he was still there yesterday morning the broadcast said.

COBRA FIREPOWER

The Bell AH-1 Cobra and the new AH1-W Super Cobra helicopters that were used so effectively by the US Marines and US Army at al-Khafji are the spearhead of their tank killing and armoured attack capability. It is a highly sophisticated weapons platform which can TOW or hurl Hellfire missiles in clumps of four to destroy a target in seconds. Besides missile power the helicopter is armed with a 3-barrel 20mm cannon, lethal to anything in its path.

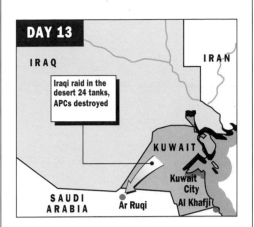

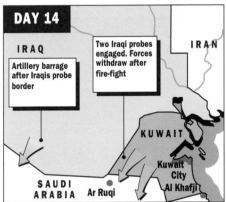

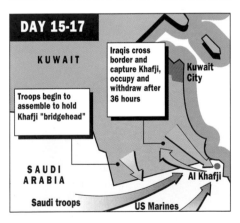

For three days the Allies were tested by the Iraqi Army, their positions probed and prodded. The attack was suicidal. It wasted men and machinery and was, to quote *Time* magazine, "a weird war". The assault was small scale, only 1,500 men and perhaps 80 tanks took part and its main aim was to take a deserted Saudi border town? Why? Perhaps Saddam wanted a propaganda victory, he was getting desperate or this was just a probing raid. "They certainly have a lot of fight left in them", said General Schwarzkopf after the operation was over.

Frog in desert mud

For the first time in battle a "Frog" missile has been fired. Again Iraq has taken the initiative - but it was probably a mistake.

The missile is a surface-to-surface type which has been used by the Soviet Army since 1966. In its Iraqi version, the SS21 can be lobbed some 40 plus miles with an accuracy of about three-quarters of a mile.

It was fired across the border into the positions of the 82nd Airborne Division but it seems to have been an isolated incident as no more were fired and the "Frog" landed harmlessly in the mud.

Spectre shot down

A C-140 Hercules, specially modified for clandestine operations, may have been shot down over occupied Kuwait. The news was leaked over CBS Television after it had been tipped off from a government source. Upwards of 18 people were on board.

US change practice on loss rates

The US Central Command will no longer give out a daily loss total. This is to stop giving away any information that might be useful to the enemy, "like search-and-rescue missions that may still be ongoing."

The logistics of the "big stick" bombing was discussed by Riyadh today. On Monday 27 B-52s dropped 455 tons of bombs on Republican Guard positions, on Tuesday 21 aircraft dropped 315 tons and on Wednesday 28 "Buffs" released 470 tons.

Day 17

Friday 1 February

The US State Department says 70 terrorists attacks have been carried out during the Gulf War against countries in the coalition against Iraq, some by groups claiming solidarity with Iraq.

Basra, Faw, Abdul Khasib and Az-Zubair were attacked by Allied aircraft during the night according to Baghdad Radio.

Iraqi Radio accuses Allied pilots of bombing civilian targets and machine-gunning people in the streets causing many deaths. Iraqi Radio labels President Bush, the British Prime Minister, John Major, President Mitterrand of France and King Fahd of Saudi Arabia, as war criminals.

The Vice-President of the United States Dan Quayle, on a visit to Britain, has a meeting with the Defence Secretary, Tom King. Both men dismiss the military significance of the Khafji fighting.

In a BBC Radio interview, Dan Quayle declines to rule out a nuclear response to any Iraqi chemical attack.

France gives its permission for US B-52 bombers to overfly its territory on missions against the Iraqis. Permission is granted for the B-52s to be refuelled by tanker aircraft using French bases.

FLYING TANKERS

The desire to maximize ordnance loads and the distances involved in many of the interdiction missions that were staged against targets in Iraq and Kuwait meant that in-flight refuelling was a routine feature of *Desert Storm*. As a consequence, some of the Allied nations assembled substantial tanker forces at a number of locations in the Gulf region and these were kept very busy, performing pre- and post-strike refuelling duties.

In the case of the US Air Force, the long-serving KC-135 Stratotanker was the main aircraft that was used and this depended upon the "flying boom" to effect the transfer of fuel. In this method, an operator in the rear of the tanker literally "plugs" a boom device into a receptacle located on the receiving aircraft.

Other services such as Britain's Royal Air Force, the US Marine Corps and the US Navy - prefer the "hose and drogue" method, whereby a basket is streamed behind the tanker and it is the responsibility of the receiver to make contact with the aid of a probe. RAF tankers in the Gulf consisted of VC-IOs and Victors while the US Marines used the KC-130 Hercules and the Navy relied on the carrierborne KA-6D Intruder.

ABOVE: *Two F-14 Tomcats refuel using the "hose and drogue" technique favoured by the US Navy and Royal Air Force.*

RIGHT: *The USAF prefers a more direct approach to refuelling. Here an F-16 plugs into a tanker for a top-up.*

Day 18

Saturday 2 February

An American intelligence spokesman, Admiral Mike McConnell, dismissed reports that two Iraqi air defence commanders have been executed on Saddam Hussein's orders because of their failure to counter Allied air attacks.

A further Scud missile strikes Israel.

A group of more than 100 Indian nurses reported missing in Iraq arrive at a refugee camp at Ruweished across the Jordanian border.

The British Foreign Secretary, Douglas Hurd, proposes a sweeping new security association in the Middle East once the war is over. He says there must be progress in the Arab-Israel dispute and more equitable sharing of the Gulf's oil wealth.

US Defense Secretary, Dick Cheney, says there will be no sanctuary for Iraqi forces inside Iraq. He says it is possible that Iraq has refrained from using chemical weapons against Israel because it knows Israel might retaliate with unconventional weapons. After the war, Mr Cheney says, the coalition forces may want to maintain some kind of international sanctions to deny Saddam Hussein the capability of rebuilding his forces. Mr Cheney rules out any ceasefire until Iraq complies with UN resolutions.

Iraqi troops being slowly sealed off in Kuwait

The Allied coalition is slowly but surely strangling the lifelines of the Iraqi troops occupying Kuwait.

Supremacy has now been gained on the sea with the Iraqi Navy being "virtually obliterated". Air supremacy has already been heralded.

The Chief of Staff at US Central Command said that Iraq was now using secondary roads and temporary pontoon bridges. Of the 30 major bridges leading into the Kuwaiti theatre of operations, 25 have been bombed and cut.

This means that transport is now backing up because of the lack of speeds attainable on the poor roads. Bottlenecks are occurring.

With air supremacy, spotter planes, which are constantly in the air, and which are known as Forward Air Patrols, can call up fire from ground artillery as well as from Marine AV 8B Harriers and USAF A-10 Thunderbolts. By strafing these convoys unhindered from Iraqi air power, more bottlenecks are caused by wrecked and damaged vehicles.

In spite of this the Allies will not be drawn on the question of when a ground offensive will begin.

It was also announced that a marine attack had been launched to clear the island of Faylakah. Though not said directly, this could point to a preparation of a full-scale amphibious assault at a later date.

The island is key to gaining a foothold in Kuwait City with Faylakah being used as first stage base for directing any landing.

There was an aerial attack last Saturday which was used to knock out the Iraqi "Silkworm" shore batteries further north in Kuwait and there is some evidence that previous attacks have happened in the past.

The concern of the American people grows day by day regarding the prisoners of war.

THEY ALSO SERVE ...

The possible capture in Khafji of a female US Marine has brought sharply into focus the role of women in war. Today the US armed forces has about 11 percent of women under arms; some estimates put 40, 000 of them in the Gulf. Their roles vary greatly from truck drivers to pilots and navigators.

The Iranians have made great efforts to exploit the propaganda value: i.e. that having women serving in the Gulf is an insult to Islamic laws. Baghdad Radio has made much play in recent days of male and female US conscripts being caught. They would all be treated "in accordance with the spirit of lofty Islamic laws".

This latest incident will also add to the debate going on in the US as congressmen get uneasy at the thought of female prisoners-of-war and the way that could turn the views of the public.

Women are serving with the British contingents as well, mainly in medical and nursing roles, but their profile is far less high than in the US military.

Day 19

Sunday 3 February

Baghdad Radio reports that over the past few days the Syrian authorities have handed over seven US pilots whose planes have been shot down by the Iraqi air defence to the American Embassy in Damascus. A US military spokesman in Saudi Arabia denies any knowledge of this report.

The Iranian newspaper the *Tehran Times,* says Iran and other Muslim counties may boycott the annual pilgrimage to Mecca in protest at the presence of US troops in Saudi Arabia.

The US ambassador in London, Henry Catto, says he does not trust promises made by the Iranian government that it will continue to hold onto Iraqi planes and pilots until the war is over. British Foreign Secretary, Douglas Hurd, says he doubts that Iran will break its promise.

One of Iran's high-ranking Shi'ite clergyman, Ayatollah Mohammed-Reza Golpayegani, warns the US of dire consequences of attacks on the Iraqi people. In a letter to President Bush he urges the withdrawal of the US troops. He also condemns Iraq's occupation of Kuwait.

Thousands of Moroccans stage a pro-Iraqi demonstration in Rabat organized by five opposition parties and Islamic fundamentalists.

SHELLS FROM THE SEA

In the early hours of 4 February, the guns of USS *Missouri* shelled shore positions in southern Kuwait. It was the classic use of naval guns to shell land positions from a distance, far out of range of enemy fire. Later *Missouri* was joined by the USS *Wisconsin*. Both ships are Iowa class battleships, carry 16 inch guns and can lob shells nearly 25 miles.

Fire is made more accurate by the use of a spotter plane that corrects the shells if they fall short. This is normally done by calling grid references to the ship. In turn, the gunners correct their bearing and angle of elevation. During the opening days of the war *Wisconsin* was also used to fire Tomahawk Cruise missiles at Iraq.

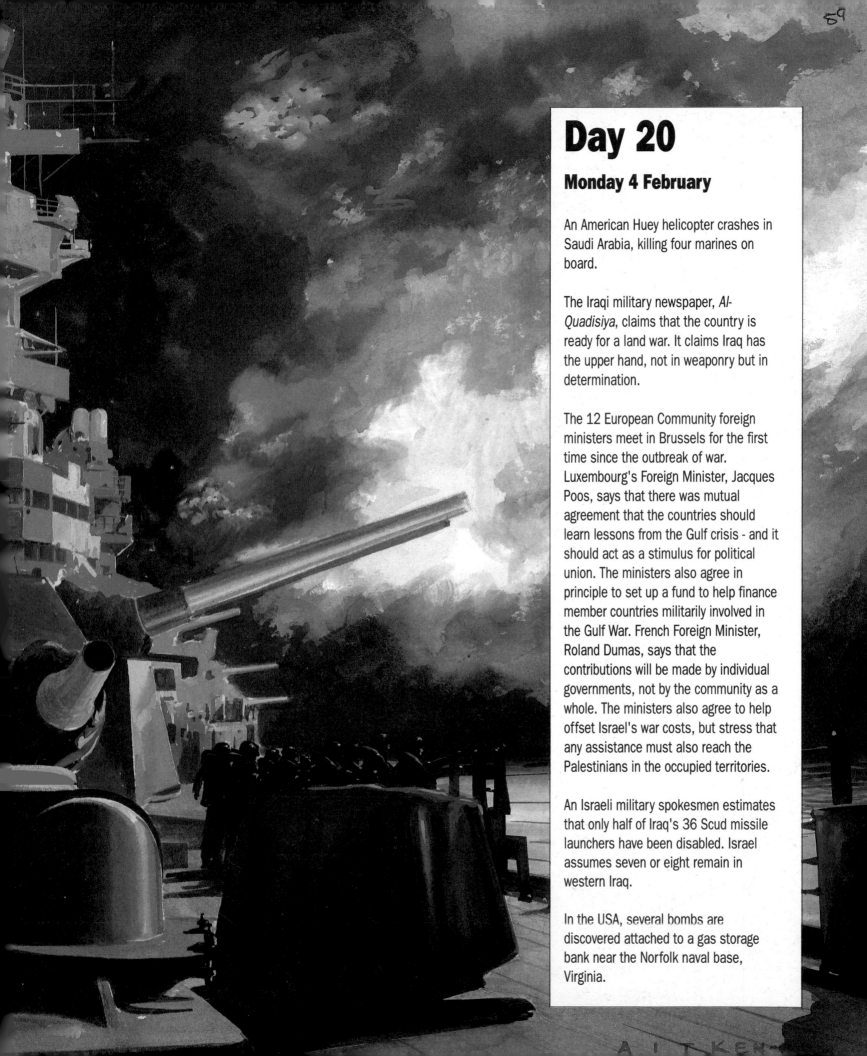

Day 20

Monday 4 February

An American Huey helicopter crashes in Saudi Arabia, killing four marines on board.

The Iraqi military newspaper, *Al-Quadisiya*, claims that the country is ready for a land war. It claims Iraq has the upper hand, not in weaponry but in determination.

The 12 European Community foreign ministers meet in Brussels for the first time since the outbreak of war. Luxembourg's Foreign Minister, Jacques Poos, says that there was mutual agreement that the countries should learn lessons from the Gulf crisis - and it should act as a stimulus for political union. The ministers also agree in principle to set up a fund to help finance member countries militarily involved in the Gulf War. French Foreign Minister, Roland Dumas, says that the contributions will be made by individual governments, not by the community as a whole. The ministers also agree to help offset Israel's war costs, but stress that any assistance must also reach the Palestinians in the occupied territories.

An Israeli military spokesmen estimates that only half of Iraq's 36 Scud missile launchers have been disabled. Israel assumes seven or eight remain in western Iraq.

In the USA, several bombs are discovered attached to a gas storage bank near the Norfolk naval base, Virginia.

Cheney and Powell fly to Gulf on President's orders

US Defense Secretary Dick Cheney and Colin Powell, Chairman of the Joint Chiefs of Staff, are flying to Saudi Arabia this week to discuss the timing of an Allied ground war with General Schwarzkopf.

The timing is crucial, for if a ground war is to be launched, it must be done before the hot weather begins, and before the holy month of Ramadan, which begins on March 17. According to the Pentagon, General Schwarzkopf is recommending a mid-February attack, nicknamed the "Valentine's Day massacre".

No decision is likely to be taken until the latest assessment (due this week) of the impact of the air bombardment on the Iraqi troops, and on the Republican Guard in particular. The Pentagon wants the Republican Guard - an elite force numbering some 150,000 - to be thoroughly weakened before exposing Allied troops to possible high casualties.

So far, intelligence reports and aerial photography indicate that many of the crack troops are sitting out the bombing in underground bunkers encased in reinforced concrete, and have lost no more than 15 percent of tanks, guns and fighting power.

Mr Bush has said that the visit by Cheney and Powell is intended in part to discuss with ground commanders whether air power alone could force the Iraqis out of Kuwait. It may be that the visit is partly in response to pressure from Congress - many members feel the air war should continue for several more months.

At the press conference, Mr Bush emphasized that he would follow the advice of his military advisers. He would not "delay for the sake of delay, hoping it would save lives".

GENERAL COLIN POWELL

General Colin Luther Powell was the link in the chain of command between President Bush and General Schwarzkopf. Born in 1937, he was the youngest ever chairman of the US joint chiefs of staff when he was appointed in 1989. He has been described as a "can do" person and has said that his greatest joy is commanding troops in the field. Having won a Purple Heart in Vietnam he was the fourth black to reach four-star rank in the US army and in 1972 was chosen from 1,500 applicants for detachment to the White House as a military adviser.

Born in Harlem in a Jamaican immigrant family, he says he owes everything to his parents, who taught him to believe in hard work and getting ahead. He married in 1962 and has one son and two daughters. His main recreation, apart from racquetball, is restoring old Volvos.

America has taken its remembrance of "the boys over there" to heart and yellow ribbons festoon America's streets.

Conditions in Iraqi cities are getting worse, say refugees

Conditions in the Iraqi cities are said to be grim. Refugees fleeing to Jordan have painted a graphic picture: they report that after 19 days of bombing the cities have no electricity or water, and that there is an acute shortage of food. Moreover, the Iraqi Oil Ministry has announced that citizens will have to do without petrol, heating oil, or cooking oil. Most fuels have in fact been in short supply since the war started.

The saturation bombing carried out has made it inevitable that civilian buildings have been struck. General Schwarzkopf has emphasized that Allied pilots are taking "extraordinary care" to avoid civilian casualties, but it has been admitted that weapons systems are not always 100 percent accurate.

There can be no doubt that conditions in cities such as Baghdad (*see above*) and Basra are extremely grim, and are likely to get worse. With bombing round the clock, normal life has already been made impossible, but the World Health Organization is now concerned that civilians may suffer even more as a result of the poor food and water supplies. Reports are already coming in of people drinking water from puddles, and with disrupted sewage systems there is an ever-growing risk of cholera and typhoid epidemics.

Day 21

Tuesday 5 February

Baghdad Radio broadcasts a series of messages, apparently in code. Several of them are described as coming from headquarters. They are followed by a call to those abroad who support revolutionary and Palestinian action to strike at the countries attacking Iraq.

US B-52 bombers begin arriving at RAF Fairford in Britain.

Luxembourg's Foreign Minister, Jacques Poos, says he expects the Gulf War will be over by the end of February. The British Foreign Office later describes this view as over-optimistic.

Czechoslovakia sends 37 more soldiers to Saudi Arabia to reinforce its anti-chemical warfare unit in the region.

En route to Iran, the Soviet Foreign Minister, Alexander Belonogov, says that the war is already exceeding reasonable limits, and that Baghdad is being damaged irreparably. He calls on the Iraqi leadership to restore Kuwait's independence.

The French Defence Minister, Pierre Joxe, speaking in Riyadh, confirms that French troops will participate in any ground offensive, including any incursion into Iraqi territory. He adds that, for certain missions, French troops will be under American control.

Iraq breaks off diplomatic relations with Allies

After 22 days into the Gulf war, Iraq has broken off diplomatic relations with Britain, the United States, France and Italy, as well as Egypt and Saudi Arabia. There has been no official report - it came via Baghdad Radio - and neither the Foreign Office in London nor the White House have been officially informed.

In fact no British or US diplomats are left in Baghdad, though in theory the embassies are still open, and the Iraq Embassy in London still has a staff of three left. In practice, the breaking off of relations will make little difference. Contact with the remaining diplomats in London had amounted simply to official complaints over breaches of the Geneva Convention regarding PoWs.

Diplomatic efforts to end the war are now focused on Tehran, where senior envoys from the Soviet Union and Turkey met Iranian leaders. Washington reacted coolly to Iran's offer to act as a mediator, but in any case there is no sign of a change of heart in Baghdad.

Turkey on the other hand has expressed support for the Iranian peace moves, though the Turks and Iranians are deeply suspicious of each other in this area. They are watching each other's moves carefully - the Turks fear that Iran might join forces with Iraq, while the Iranians fear that Turkey intends to gain control of the northern area of Iraq just across its border, including the oil-rich town of Kirkuk.

A French Mirage 2000 stands ready for action on its desert ramp.

US shot down fleeing planes

It has just been announced in Riyadh that the US Air Force has shot down four Iraqi Air Force SU-25 aircraft after they were picked up on radar and seen to be moving towards the Iranian border.

It is the first time that the Allies have shot down aircraft attempting to flee over to Iran. They came in for considerable criticism that they had done nothing to prevent upwards of 142 aircraft fleeing into Iran.

In response to that criticism, the Pentagon assured observers that any hostile act on the part of the Iraqis would be met with similar action by the Allies.

There are a number of ways that these aircraft could have been spotted, from conventional AWACs activity, whereby all hostile air space is continuously monitored, to conventional radar.

Emergency aid on its way to Iraq

The United Nations has announced that it is to send emergency medical aid to the mothers and children of Iraq. It will be delivered by representatives of the World Health Organization and the UN Children's Fund. A Swiss Red Cross envoy has arrived in Baghdad, bringing with him 19 tons of medical supplies.

THE STEALTHY BLACK JET

Seldom seen by day, Lockheed's remarkable F-117A was one of the undoubted stars of the Gulf War and about 40 examples of the celebrated "Stealth Fighter" were deployed to the region for *Desert Storm*. Virtually undetectable by radar, they were able to operate with impunity and succeeded in wreaking havoc on a grand scale. In view of that, it was hardly surprising that pilots of the 37th Tactical Fighter Wing - the USAF's only "stealth" outfit - drew the hardest and, in theory at least, the best-defended targets, one notable early success occurring in "downtown" Baghdad when an F-117A lobbed a 2,000 lb bomb through the roof of the Iraqi Air Force headquarters building.

"Stealth" characteristics are only part of the story though, for it isn't a lot of good having an aircraft that is invisible if it can't accurately put bombs on targets. Fortunately, the "Black Jet" does possess that ability, being fully compatible with laser-guided weaponry and that's another reason why it drew the high-value targets like command and control centres in and around Baghdad. Commenting on the F-117A, a senior USAF officer remarked, "There basically is nothing else that we're using for attacks on Baghdad. The F-117 is doing the work for us."

After the war is over...

US Secretary of State, James Baker, testified before the House of Rep-representatives Foreign Affairs Committee and outlined his main ideas for a region-wide peace after the war has ended.

This included help with rebuilding Iraq and allowing Iraq to have a peace-making as well as a peacekeeping role in the Gulf.

America would not be seeking a full-time presence in the Gulf area, but all military proliferation would be controlled and monitored.

He stressed that Israel should be reconciled with its Arab neighbours and that the US would reduce its dependency on Middle Eastern oil output.

Day 22

Wednesday 6 February

British sources announce that British minesweepers are being moved into the northern Gulf over the next few days to clear Iraqi mines. A BBC correspondent says this would be essential preparation for any Allied amphibious assault on Kuwait.

Arriving in Tehran, the Soviet deputy Foreign Minister, Alexander Belonogov, states that his country and Iran are maintaining close contacts, since they both want to see an end to bloodshed in the Gulf.

An Allied military briefing in Saudi Arabia reports a change of tactics by American F-16 fighter bombers in their raids on Iraqi Republican Guard and tank formations. The F-16 pilots have switched from using conventional bombs to infra-red guided Maverick missiles.

A Qatari owned cargo vessel, the *Fatah al Khier* carrying explosives and mines to Saudi Arabia, is refused permission by Egypt to pass through the Suez Canal.

US President Bush, assures Pakistan's Prime Minister, Nawaz Sharif, that coalition forces will maintain the sanctity of Iraq's holy places.

Sri Lankan Foreign Minister, Harold Herat, says his country is opening its ports and airports for Allied refuelling purposes, and to assist in the repatriation of war refugees.

LYNX AND SEA SKUA

Royal Navy Lynx helicopters with Sea Skua missiles proved a devastating combination during *Desert Storm*.

Built by British Aerospace, the eight-foot Sea Skua rocket weighs only 320 lbs and the Lynx can carry up to four on board. They are ideal against small fast targets such as the gun boats and patrol craft of the Iraqi Navy.

Operating from the Northern Gulf, the Navy almost single-handedly annihilated Iraq's small maritime force.

Targets can be located either from an outside source such as an AWAC or ship, or by using the helicopter's own sensors. These include the "Orange Crop" electronic emission sensors or the helicopter's 180 degree Sea Spray Mk 1 radar. "Orange Crop" has identify, active search, or fire control radars and will give the helicopter clues to identify a particular target. The Sea Spray radar needs to be used sparingly as it can give away the helicopter. Climbing quickly to get the maximum benefit from a single sweep, the radar on the Lynx can identify a target, lock-on and fire its missile. Sea Skua then drops away from the helicopter, skims over the sea and hits its target.

The Lynx from HMS London *was one of four Sea Skua armed Lynx helicopters that flew patrols in the Gulf during the war. It is seen here resting on the deck of RFA* Argus (*below*) *and flying point duty in front of the RN Gulf flagship, HMS* London.

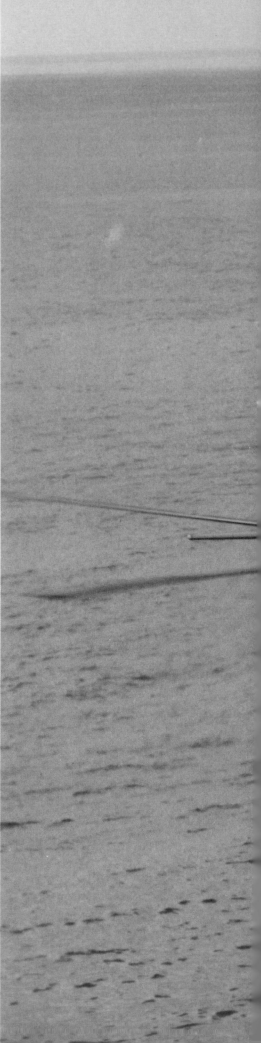

Day 23

Thursday 7 February

President Bush says that the road to peace will be long and tough but an Allied victory will offer a historic opportunity to bring peace to the Gulf region. He concedes that the impact of the Gulf crisis has deepened the recession in the US economy.

USAF tankers have arrived at Mont de Marsan airfield in south-west France. They will assist the midair refuelling of B-52s from RAF Fairford.

Soviet deputy Foreign Minister, Alexander Belonogov, holds talks with Iranian Foreign Minister, Ali Akbar Velayati, and other ministers in Tehran. The Soviet side expresses satisfaction with Iran's neutrality. The Soviet news agency TASS says Iran should reject attempts to turn the conflict into a war between Christianity and Islam.

The Iranian authorities report heavy bombardment last night of the Iraqi cities of Zorbatiya and Ta'an near the Iranian border.

The British military commander, General Sir Peter de la Billière, says he believes a ground offensive is inevitable. Before it begins, he says, there will be massive and unrelenting air strikes.

The Iranian news agency says six more Iraqi military aircraft have flown into Iranian air space but only one managed to land safely. One pilot was killed.

Iraqi Army begins to desert in droves - bombing is working

After weeks of Allied bombing, Iraqi soldiers are beginning to desert. They are surrendering to Allied soldiers, and even, as reported today, to journalists.

An English journalist from the *Independent* has given an incredible report of how four Iraqi soldiers appeared out of nowhere as he and his colleagues drove across the desert, close to the Kuwait-Saudi border. At first, the party of journalists - two British, from the *Independent*, and two Americans from *Life* magazine - thought they were Syrian soldiers.

It was only when the soldiers held up white pieces of paper that the reporters realized that these were Iraqis wanting to surrender. US aircraft have been dropping leaflets, printed in Arabic, telling Iraqi soldiers to give themselves up - and that is exactly what this four did, holding up the leaflets as flags of surrender.

The story that emerged is pathetic. These soldiers, like many in the Iraqi army, are conscripts, unwilling and untrained, who have been trying to survive life at the front under the relentless daily bombardment from the Allies. For two months they had been living dug into a narrow foxhole. They were unshaven, unwashed, and very hungry. Their uniforms were dirty and frayed, and their boots were split. They were fed once a day, on a bowl of rice and some bread.

Anyone who tried to escape was shot at by the Republican Guards, who in effect are hemming-in these front-line troops and preventing them either surrendering to the enemy, or deserting and returning home. These men had escaped after dark, and had then walked all night across the desert. Mines are planted everywhere, to prevent soldiers escaping. These soldiers were lucky because they knew the minefields and so were able to make their way across.

They said most Iraqi soldiers felt the

AMERICA IN MOURNING

The troops are beginning to come home. As heroes, but not smiling and waving greetings to their loved ones. They are arriving in metal caskets shipped over by MAC into eastern seaboard airbases to be met by family and honour guard. These are the first casualties of *Desert Storm*. Mercifully very few so far, but one too many as far as the families are concerned. Within a few days they will be buried with the honour and respect due to them. But how many more will come home this way?

same - that Saddam should never have gone into Kuwait, and they insisted that everyone would surrender once the ground war started. The Republican Guard are different of course. They are young, well-trained, and well disciplined - basically they will do what Saddam Hussein tells them.

It was the relentless bombing campaign that drove these men to surrender, and soon that bombardment will get worse as the focus of the campaign is switched to the area around Kuwait City. Already the "Buffs" are bombing nearer the border.

Day 24

Friday 8 February

The commander of the US forces in the Gulf, General Norman Schwarzkopf, says it is too early to tell if a ground war is needed.

The Iranians say another 215 people, mainly Sudanese and Vietnamese, have crossed into Iran from Iraq.

Holland announces that it is to supply Israel with eight Patriot launchers.

British Naval Authorities say one of their helicopters has destroyed an Iraqi patrol boat in the northern Gulf. About ten survivors were seen making their way towards Faylakah Island in a life raft.

British Defence Secretary, Tom King, says between 15 to 20 per cent of Iraq's fighting capacity in the Kuwait area has been destroyed.

In London, Kurdish political groups say Iraqi soldiers have been surrendering to Kurdish guerillas in the far north of Iraq. They say that as many as 80,000, many of them Kurds, have deserted so far.

A senior French Foreign Ministry official, François Scheer, holds talks in Syria on the Gulf War with the Foreign Minister, Farouq al-Shara, and Vice-President Abdel Halim Khaddam.

Italy agrees to let the Allies use an airport near Milan as a base for the tankers that refuel fighter aircraft.

War costs money as well as lives

Amid all the diplomatic negotiations, political manoeuvering and moral agonizing, it is easy to forget that wars cost money - an unbelievable amount of money. Modern, high-tech warfare costs millions - whatever money it is expressed in. Missiles and "smart bombs" are very costly fireworks. The troops, aircraft, armour and equipment all existed already, but deploying them in the Gulf, with all the ancillary communications centres, supply systems and field hospitals, was an expensive business.

The cost of Britain's deployment in the Gulf is estimated at £1.25 billion for the current financial year. To date, Britain has been offered £370 million from Germany, £300 million from Saudi Arabia, and £26 million from Japan.

Last night, however, the Kuwaiti government-in-exile promised Britain £660 million towards the cost of forcing Saddam Hussein out of Kuwait. The offer came after Douglas Hurd, the British Foreign Secretary, held talks with the exiled Emir of Kuwait, Sheikh Jabir al-Ahmed al-Sabah, and the Crown Prince, Sheikh Saad al-Abdullah al-Sabah, in Taif, a mountain resort in Saudi Arabia.

Mr Hurd was visiting Saudi Arabia as part of his Middle East tour, and is quoted as saying: "We had an obligation to react to the invasion of Kuwait as we have, but the costs are very high and this contribution will help significantly towards the achievement of our objectives."

It is evident that a massive build-up is taking place along the Kuwaiti and Saudi-Arabian borders with Iraq.

Baghdad suffers

Baghdad has been taking a pasting from bombs and missiles - and most of the suffering has fallen on civilians. That was the message Western newspapers were receiving from their reporters in the city. Although the markets seemed busy, food was scarce and expensive, water was a problem in some areas, and there was no electricity. Hotels could no longer provide food (the decent food that Western journalists were accustomed to, anyway). Guests were trying to cook in their rooms, using gas appliances, charcoal, paraffin lamps, even candles.

During the first weeks of the war military and strategic sites had been the targets: by the fourth week, bridges and roads were being bombed. In either case, whatever the intended targets may have been, Western journalists were emphasizing damage to mosques, hospitals, and residential areas, and civilian casualties, especially children.

The reports seemed truthful enough, but how accurate may never be known. A traditional intelligence principle says that victories and successes should be reported loud and clear, but defeats and losses should be treated as secret and communicated in code. Civilian suffering, on the other hand, is an international public relations weapon: it should be exaggerated and publicized. Most Western journalists' reports from Baghdad and from inside Iraq carried the rider that they had been subjected to Iraqi censorship and restrictions on movement, and many of them stressed that Iraqi officials had been eager to display the effects of the Allied bombardment on civilian areas.

President Saddam is said, during this week, to have told a visiting Arab diplomat: "We built this country in 20 years. Now we are more advanced. We can rebuild it in five."

US citizens told to leave Jordan

The State Department in Washington has sent an urgent message, urging all US citizens to leave Jordan immediately - there are estimated to be some 4,000 US citizens there. The US Embassy has also been ordered to send home 10 staff. Non-essential staff and families were advised to leave weeks ago.

The US move came as a surprise to the Jordanian authorities, and suggests that the Allies are about to launch a new offensive.

EYES IN THE SKY

Airborne early warning (AEW) operations can in broad terms be said to fall into two major areas of activity, namely offensive and defensive. In the latter, AEW-dedicated aircraft such as the Boeing E-4 Sentry function as flying "pickets", orbiting at altitude in order to extend the coverage of ground radars and alert other defensive elements such as fighter interceptors to the presence of incoming hostile warplanes. In the latter, they use their radar sensors to observe air activity over the battlefield, advising friendly echelons of enemy air activity. In instances where enemy fighters look as if they pose a threat, the E-3 crews can instruct air superiority fighters to intervene and see off that threat. It is also helpful to notify attack assets of the absence of threats for they are then able to take their time in executing an attack and, in so doing, can usually accomplish their objectives much more effectively.

During the course of *Desert Shield* and *Desert Storm*, both of these tasks were performed with conspicuous success, US Air Force and Royal Saudi Air Force Sentries maintaining constant surveillance of friendly and enemy airspace. Indeed, many of these Iraqi warplanes that were destroyed in air combat could not have been shot down without instructions and data that originated from the AEW component.

Elsewhere, carrier-borne Grumman E-7C Hawkeyes (*see below*) provided similar support to the US Navy battle groups that were operating in the Red Sea and the Gulf.

Day 25

Saturday 9 February

An Iraqi Scud missile attack is made against Israel, with at least three explosions above Tel Aviv. A Patriot missile is fired to intercept the missile. About 25 people are injured.

An official Syrian newspaper, *al-Thawra*, urges Iraqis to assassinate Saddam Hussein to end the war.

US marine spokesman, General Richard Neal, says more than 750 Iraqi tanks are confirmed destroyed as well as slightly fewer armoured personnel carriers and artillery pieces. He says a Silkworm missile site has been destroyed by UN naval forces.

The deputy commander of the French ground forces, General Daniel Gazeau, says the French are fully integrated into the Allied operation, and liaison with the US is good at all levels.

President Gorbachev says events have taken a dramatic turn. The recent military action means there is a threat of the UN mandate being overstepped. He says the war is causing great concern in the Soviet Union - especially as it is raging along Soviet borders.

A Red Cross convoy carrying ten tons of medical aid crosses into Iraq from Iran.

Iran appeals to UNESCO to help protect religious and cultural sites in Iraq.

HEAVY METAL MOVER

Amongst all the shiny new high-tech kit employed in the air war against Iraq was a lumbering brute of a machine, which had just completed 30 years service with the United States Air Force. Despite its status as a veteran, Boeing's Stratofortress, more familiarly known to generations of Strategic Air Command personnel as the "Buff", was soon put into action and once again proved its worth as a bomb carrier and deliverer.

While it is now capable of employing precision weapons for pinpoint attacks against hard targets, in the war against Iraq the B-52G version appears to have been used purely for saturation bombing. In this concept of operation, it generally operates in "cells" of three aircraft so as to maximize destructive potential across a wide area. Since each B-52G can carry 51 M-117 750 lb "iron" bombs, it doesn't take much imagination to realize the psychological impact on anyone unlucky enough to be in the target area when an unseen and unheard "cell" begins unloading. Within a few seconds, just over 50 tons of ordnance can be disgorged and those on the receiving end will have little or no warning of its arrival.

During *Desert Storm* B-52 operations were conducted from a number of bases. Some were close to the war zone, allowing two sorties a day to be flown by each aircraft; others were several thousand miles away, at locations like Moron, in Spain and RAF Fairford in England. It was from the latter base that a total of 58 sorties was flown during the period 9 to 28 February, each sortie typically lasting from 14 to 17 hours, highlighted by a few tense moments as weapons release neared. In those 58 sorties, the 806th Bomb Wing (Provisional) dropped some 2.2 million pounds of bombs, but that was only a small fraction of the ordnance delivered by the mighty "Buff" in seven weeks of war.

LEFT: *A B-52G thunders away from RAF Fairford in southern England. The base was reactivated at short notice as a station for the SAC bombers after France agreed to allow non-nuclear-carrying bombers to overfly her territory.*

Day 26

Sunday 10 February

Saddam Hussein addresses the nation for the first time in two weeks and says victory is assured. He says Iraq is determined to fight on and praises the countries and people standing by Iraq, among others, Jordan, Sudan and the Palestinians. President Bush says that he did not hear a word about withdrawing from Kuwait in Saddam Hussein's speech.

US Defense Secretary, Dick Cheney, speaking to correspondents during the flight home from Saudi Arabia, says the Allied air offensive has caused serious damage to Iraq's military capability. He says it will be a long time before Iraq will be a threat to its neighbours.

US officials say a desalination plant at Safaniya in Saudi Arabia has been reopened. It has been closed due to the drifting oil slick.

Dick Cheney says the Allied campaign against Iraq is going well. Iraq's air force is believed to be ineffective, its air defences degraded and its navy nonexistent. Production facilities for nuclear, biological and chemical weapons have been mostly destroyed although Iraq retains significant amounts of chemical weapons. He stresses there can be no pause in the campaign - it will continue until Iraq is forced out of Kuwait or withdraws.

A BBC correspondent says that two bridges in Baghdad were destroyed during the night.

Bush orders bombing campaign to continue - but land offensive is near says Washington

Speculation is growing that the start of the ground offensive is near. Today, US Defense Secretary Dick Cheney and General Colin Powell will report to President Bush after their fact-finding trip to the Gulf, which included talks with Commander-in-Chief Norman Schwarzkopf on the current situation.

Cheney is reported as claiming that air attacks had been very successful, saying they had destroyed "a very significant part of what was the world's fourth largest army. I don't think it's the world's fourth largest army any more."

However, reports indicate that military commanders recommended that the air war should go on for at least another two weeks. They believe that an early ground offensive without more intensive bombing would lead to heavy US casualties. Some commanders have even recommended that the bombardment should last another month.

Further bombing is also favoured by British public opinion. Prime Minister John Major has underlined the British commitment to continue the air bombardment.

The reluctance to start a ground war is based on the assessment of the effect of the air campaign so far. In spite of Cheney's remarks, after three and a half weeks of air bombardment most of Iraq's army is still intact, and the Pentagon believes that Iraqi positions in Kuwait have been largely unaffected by the campaign.

So far estimates are that 750 tanks, 650 guns and 600 APCs (armoured personnel carriers) have been destroyed - approximately 20 percent. But only one out of eight divisions of the Republican Guard has been destroyed. More damage must be inflicted on the Guard if heavy US casualties are to be avoided.

Aerial reconnaisance by both Royal Saudi Air Force and USAF E-3 Sentries has established that many thousands of these crack Iraqi troops are sitting out the Allied bombing in deep underground bunkers covered with reinforced concrete. The bunkers are thought to be proof against everything, except the laser-guided "smart" bombs which could be guided down the small ventilation shafts.

The recent pounding of the Guard by B-52s, which have been dropping thousands of bombs on these targets, has not been as effective as hoped. A saturation bombing campaign, by day and night, can now be expected in the run-up to the ground campaign.

Another factor in the decision is that the White House and the US generals are keen to delay the start of a ground war until all their forces are in position: only a few days ago tanks arrived in Saudi ports.

Buttons seen on a stand in California testify to the spirit pervading all the Allied nations at this time. But everyone was wondering when the ground offensive would start.

An American Army serviceman peers over the edge of his MRL - multiple rocket launcher- inscribed between the twin mouths. These MRLs can be found in many arsenals of the coalition armies; they deliver a powerful artillery barrage and are being used hourly to bombard Iraqi front-line positions.

Day 27

Monday 11 February

A civil defence spokesman in Basra says that more than 200 civilians have been killed in bomb attacks on the city.

A Soviet parliamentary leader Alexander Dzasokhov, underlines Soviet concern about the scale of Allied action against Iraq. He stresses in a BBC interview that the war should not harm the improved relations between Moscow and Washington. He says that the Soviet Union feels a ceasefire would give a chance for all sides to reassess the situation.

Turkish Foreign Minister, Ahmet Kurtcebe Alptemocin, begins a tour of Syria, Egypt and Saudi Arabia, to re-affirm that his government has no designs on Iraqi territory. He begins his visit in Damascus. On his arrival, the Syrian Foreign Minister, Farouq al-Shara, says the security in the Gulf region is a matter for the states in the area, not the outsiders.

An Israeli military spokesman reports that another missile has been fired at Israel. The missile hits a residential area, injures seven people, and damages houses.

Iraqi Minister for Religious Affairs, Abdullah Fadel, says thousands of Iraqi civilians have been killed or wounded in Allied air attacks. He says mosques, churches and dozens of houses in the three holy Shi'ite cities have been destroyed.

SIR PETER DE LA BILLIERE

Lieutenant-General Sir Peter Edgar de la Cour de la Billière was appointed commander of the British Forces in the Middle East on 1 October 1990. He is the British army's most decorated officer, with a Military Cross gained when leading an assault in Oman in 1959, a Bar for undercover operations in Aden in 1966, a DSO in 1976, and a CBE in 1983. He was knighted in 1988. He has been variously described as cool, clear-headed, steely, and with a streak of ruthlessness. Much of his career has been spent with the SAS, which under his direction during the late 1970s developed into the awesome counter-terrorist and undercover military force that operates today. He was one of those who predicted, even before the ground war started, that it would be over quickly with only a few Allied casualties. Aged 57, he is married and has three children. His recreations include squash, farming, sailing, and "being with his family".

Arms dealers to Iraq will be prosecuted in Germany

Bonn is to prosecute at least nine firms for violations of the arms embargo against Iraq. Hans-Dietrich Genscher, the German Foreign Minister, has admitted that German firms illegally sold military equipment to Iraq.

There have now been allegations that a further nine firms, including Thyssen, have been helping Iraq to build a chemical warfare laboratory. Bonn is now to impose tough new controls. A Customs Criminal Office is to be set up. Suspected companies will have their mail intercepted and opened, and their telephones tapped. The minimum sentence will also be raised from six months to one year.

THE FIRST FOUR WEEKS

The campaign of the first four weeks was primarily one of gaining air supremacy. The opening move was a massive air strike at targets in and around Baghdad as well as over the whole of the Iraqi theatre; a devastating blitz that used both conventional bombs as well as Tomahawk Cruise missiles launched from land and sea. Raids took place from all points of the compass. There was extensive use made of the F-117 "stealth" fighter.

The mystery of 142 plus aircraft which had "defected" to Iran remained unresolved (it was to do so until the end of the war). Much debate ensued with Iran insisting to both American and British delegates that the planes would be impounded.

Throughout the month Iraq used its Scud missiles to great effect with strikes on both Israel and Saudi Arabia. This was in spite of a concerted effort by the Allies to hunt the launchers down and destroy them. Although there was less of a threat after a few weeks, the Scuds had not been totally eradicated and continued to be a source of trouble which was as much political as military in significance.

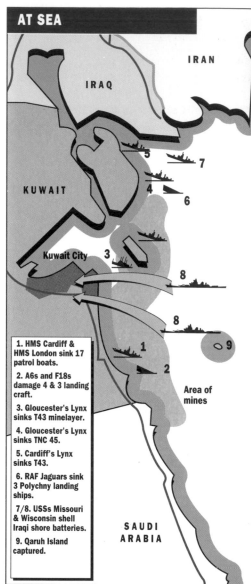

AT SEA

1. HMS Cardiff & HMS London sink 17 patrol boats.

2. A6s and F18s damage 4 & 3 landing craft.

3. Gloucester's Lynx sinks T43 minelayer.

4. Gloucester's Lynx sinks TNC 45.

5. Cardiff's Lynx sinks T43.

6. RAF Jaguars sink 3 Polychny landing ships.

7/8. USSs Missouri & Wisconsin shell Iraqi shore batteries.

9. Qaruh Island captured.

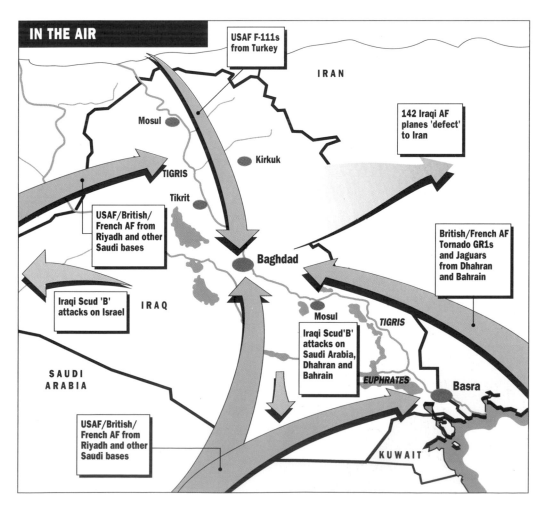

IN THE AIR

USAF F-111s from Turkey

142 Iraqi AF planes 'defect' to Iran

USAF/British/French AF from Riyadh and other Saudi bases

Iraqi Scud 'B' attacks on Israel

British/French AF Tornado GR1s and Jaguars from Dhahran and Bahrain

Iraqi Scud'B' attacks on Saudi Arabia, Dhahran and Bahrain

USAF/British/French AF from Riyadh and other Saudi bases

Activity at sea was also air orientated. US Carrier Air Wings were in action alongside British Royal Navy helicopters. In combined operations they succeeded in destroying or crippling over 90 per cent of the Iraqi Navy.

In a precursor to an amphibious invasion Allied warships began minesweeping operations in the Northern Gulf and the USSs *Wisconsin* and *Missouri* started to shell occupied Kuwait.

The land war developed into a guessing game, with movements all along the Saudi-Kuwaiti borders.

The most serious incident occurred when Iraqi troops launched a cross-border raid at Khafji, infiltrating some 10 miles into Saudi Arabia. It took Saudi and Quatari troops, supported by units of US Marines, two days for the Iraqis to be dislodged.

At the end of the month a military powwow took place between Colin Powell, Dick Cheney and General Schwarzkopf to discuss a date for the imminent ground offensive.

Day 28

Tuesday 12 February

Iraqi deputy Prime Minister, Saadoun Hammadi, speaking in Tunis, says morale is high in Iraq and that it is ready for a land battle. He later departs for Algeria.

The chairman of the Kuwaiti Information Bureau in Dhahran, Saqr al-Buayjan, alleges that Iraqi troops in Kuwait are continuing to commit atrocities.

Soviet envoy, Yevgeny Primakov, has talks in Iraq with Saddam Hussein who gives him a message outlining his position. Saddam Hussein says Moscow is involved in the crimes of the Allies because it backed the UN resolution authorizing military action. He says he is still ready to co-operate with Moscow and others in seeking an honourable solution to the problems of the region. Mr Primakov is then taken to parts of Baghdad hit by bombing. Baghdad Radio quotes him as being appalled that residential districts have been targeted.

Pakistan's Prime Minister, Nawaz Sharif, holds talks in Morocco with King Hassan on his six-point peace plan.

Jordanian officials say Syria and Yemen are to supply Jordan with oil to offset shortages caused by the Gulf crisis.

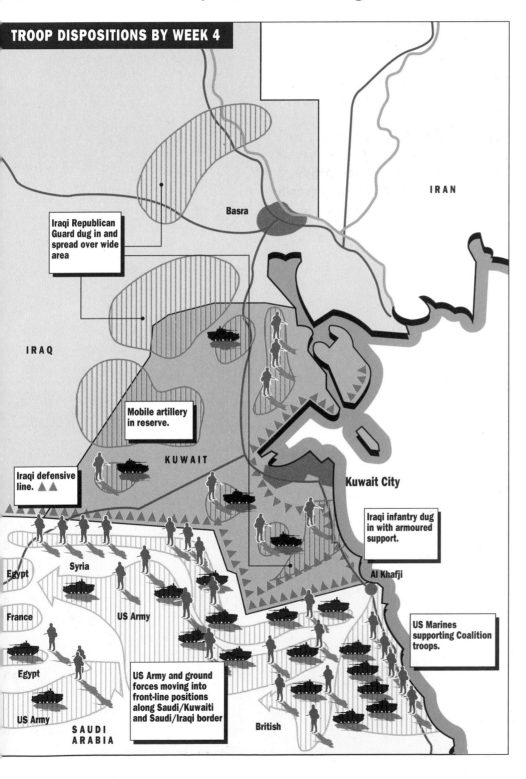

TROOP DISPOSITIONS BY WEEK 4

IRAN

Basra

Iraqi Republican Guard dug in and spread over wide area

IRAQ

Mobile artillery in reserve.

KUWAIT

Iraqi defensive line. ▲▲

Kuwait City

Iraqi infantry dug in with armoured support.

Egypt

Syria

Al Khafji

France

US Army

US Marines supporting Coalition troops.

Egypt

US Army and ground forces moving into front-line positions along Saudi/Kuwaiti and Saudi/Iraqi border

US Army

SAUDI ARABIA

British

74

TANK BUSTER

When it came to dealing with Iraq's substantial array of armoured fighting vehicles, the Allies were fortunate enough to possess a number of options. Helicopters figured prominently in the anti-armour battle but conventional aircraft also had a part to play, with the formidable A-10A Thunderbolt II ranging far and wide over the battlefield in search of targets.

As far as destroying tanks is concerned, the A-10, or "Wart Hog" as it is more familiarly known, is able to employ a number of weapons and the pilot's choice would largely be dependent upon the situation in the operating area. In the Gulf War, cluster bomb units seem to have been extensively used, these possessing a fairly large lethal "footprint". If delivered accurately they would be particularly effective against a column of tanks in close order. The AGM-65 Maverick air-to-surface missile could also be used although this is perhaps a rather expensive way of taking out a tank.

Day 29

Wednesday 13 February

The Soviet Communist Party newspaper, *Pravda,* denies Western reports that Soviet military units are serving with front-line units in Iraq.

The Iranian news agency reports that towns and cities in eastern Iraq came under heavy bombing attacks from planes last night.

The mayor of Athens, Antonis Tritsis, who has just returned from Baghdad, warns of the risk of an epidemic breaking out there. He believes many ancient monuments reaching back to Biblical times have been damaged by bombs. He says he and other mayors from historic cities in the eastern Mediterranean and the Middle East are trying to get electricity restored in Baghdad.

Iraq's deputy Prime Minister, Saadoun Hammadi, asks Morocco to withdraw its troops from Saudi Arabia in a meeting in Morocco with King Hassan.

A German government spokesman says his country is to give Israel $100 million (US dollars) to buy Patriot rockets to counter Iraqi Scud missile attacks.

Afghan sources say a second group of Mujahadeen guerrillas, led by Colonel Mohammed Qasim, is to go to Saudi Arabia to fight under Saudi command in the Gulf War.

Bunker bombing kills "400". It was "military" says Washington

The world was stunned by the news that yesterday at 4.30 am Baghdad time US bombs had hit a civilian bunker in a residential suburb to the north of Baghdad. Viewers watched in horror as TV screens showed blackened corpses, shrivelled by the intense heat, being carried out of the smouldering rubble, while weeping relatives milled about. So far, 235 bodies have been recovered.

Approximately 400 people, mainly women and children, had been sheltering in the bunker from the intensive bombing. Eye witnesses explained that local people had been sheltering there every night since the bombing campaign started, taking blankets, pillows and food supplies with them. These people had obviously thought they were safe here, in this purpose-built nuclear-proof shelter, with reinforced concrete walls 10 foot thick.

But the laser--guided bombs had found the bunker's weak point, a ventilation shaft, opening up a path to the enormous bunker below. No one stood a chance, and it is understood that there are few survivors - firemen spent 4 hours in the smoking ruin trying to cut through the tangled metal to the bunker below with oxyacetylene equipment.

Entire families may have died in this bunker, which the Iraqis claim was a

SMART BOMBS AND SMART WEAPONS?

One of the most impressive aspects of *Desert Storm* must surely have been the performance of that class of ordnance which is generally referred to as "smart weaponry".

The key to any "smart weapon" lies in its terminal guidance system which can vary considerably. Much was made of laser-guided bombs and missiles which are dependent upon a laser beam being used to "paint" the objective. In the case of bombs, they are lobbed into a beam of reflected laser energy, whereupon control fins guide the weapon to its target. The key here relates to bomb release - if they find the beam there is a high probability of a direct hit; if they don't find the beam, they won't hit the target. It's that simple, but it does call for very precise flying skills.

Bombs may also be delivered with the assistance of TV or Imaging Infra-Red (IIR) seeker heads, these devices usually being referred to as glide bombs. In this instance, the weapon system operator monitors a cockpit display which shows him pictures transmitted from the bomb's seeker head. Precise steering commands are given via a jam-resistant data link.

Equally impressive are the HARM (High-speed Anti-Radiation Missile) and ALARM (Air-Launched Anti-Radiation Missile). Both home on emissions from hostile radars but ALARM has a unique loiter mode, whereby it climbs to altitude, deploys a parachute and almost literally "hangs around" while it looks for a target to home in on.

These weapons are usually delivered from aircraft but also may be ground launched. The Tomahawk Cruise Missile is such a weapon, which when launched

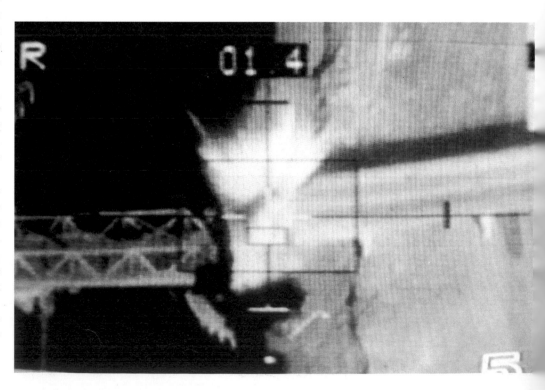

civilian shelter, and which the US say was a military command and control centre. Later, at a briefing, US spokesman Brigadier-General Neal said it was plausible that Saddam had deliberately placed women and children in the bunker, because the US had said it would not attack civilian targets. The US insist that the bunker was a legitimate military target, though later it was admitted that it had been attacked because it was believed key military personnel were sheltering there.

The incident has caused widespread revulsion in the West, as well as sparking off a wave of Arab denunciations and anti-American feeling. In Jordan, stones and paint were hurled at the US Embassy.

It now seems certain that target lists will be revized in an attempt to avoid further civilian casualties; and the whole topic of the Allied bombing campaign is certain to be raised when the European Parliament meets in Strasbourg next week.

More Allied losses

In the Riyadh military briefing the US Marine spokesman, General Richard Neal admitted that another US aircraft had been lost in combat. The total Allied air losses are now 27.

He added that the Allies have now destroyed 1,300 out of 4,200 Iraqi tank forces as well as over a third of its artillery pieces.

Day 30

Thursday 14 February

The US ambassador to the UN, Thomas Pickering, says Saddam Hussein is responsible for Iraq's civilian casualties.

The Jordanian government issues a statement condemning the massacre of civilians in the Baghdad bunker. It announces three days of mourning for the victims. Hundreds of people march on the US embassy in Amman to voice their protests.

President Gorbachev has talks in Moscow with the Kuwaiti Foreign Minister, Sheikh Sabah al-Ahmed al-Sabah, to discuss a peaceful solution to the Gulf conflict. Sheikh al-Sabah says that Moscow will have a part to play in any post-war settlement in the region.

In the Israeli-occupied territories, Palestinians begin a three day strike to mourn the victims of the Baghdad bunker bombing. In southern Lebanon Palestinians at the Ain al-Hilwe refugee camp stage a strike at the Baghdad deaths.

President Rafsanjani sends a message to UN Secretary General, Javier Pérez de Cuéllar, saying Saddam Hussein has turned down the peace initiative put forward by Iran. The message is delivered by Iran's permanent representative to the UN, Kamal Kharrazi.

(it may be land, sea or even air), drops down below the radar horizon and seeks out pre-programmed co-ordinates from which it computes its course to its target. Often hugging the ground at 100 feet or less, it hits its target with uncanny precision.

Two illustrations of the Allies' precision bombing techniques. (Left) a bridge is blown up by a laser-guided bomb from a French Jaguar and (below), a Baghdad Ministry building targeted by a USAF F-117, using a glide bomb.

Saddam offers "peace" if ...
Soviets hail an important step

On the eve of Tariq Aziz's arrival in Moscow, Baghdad radio broadcast a statement in which, without naming Kuwait, Iraq announced its willingness to comply with UN Resolution 660, withdrawing to positions it held on 1 August. Initially, the announcement was greeted with jubilation, especially in Iraq itself. Then it became clear that the Iraqis at the same time had elaborated a long list of impossible conditions, including an immediate end to hostilities, rescinding all other UN resolutions on Kuwait, ending the blockade, Israel's withdrawal from the occupied territories, democracy in Kuwait, economic reparations to Iraq, together with the cancellation of all debts, and finally, the conclusion of a security agreement for the Gulf which would exclude all foreign forces.

The announcement succeeded in forcing the United States and its more belligerent allies onto the defensive, threatening for the first time to divide the coalition. Egypt's firm rejection of the offer, demanding unconditional withdrawal, calmed many nerves.

The Russians, of course, understood the broadcast within the context of their diplomacy, and were encouraged. The Soviet Foreign Minister, Alexander Bessmertnykh, was reported to have said that it opened "a new chapter in the history of the conflict. This is an important beginning."

From the outset of the Gulf Crisis, the Soviet Union tried to fashion a diplomatic solution, using its long-standing ties with the Iraqi leadership to urge withdrawal, while at the same time hoping that "the new world order" would enable it to restrain the United States. Foreign Minister Shevardnadze and Gorbachev's personal adviser, Yevgeny Primakov, whose knowledge and understanding of Iraqi politics was second to none, began intensive and protracted efforts through October and November to construct an Arab solution to withdrawal from Kuwait. At the centre of this policy lay the mistaken conviction that the crisis would not end in war: a conviction which proved to be an illusion with the first bombing raids on Baghdad.

The second Soviet diplomatic initiative began on the eve of the ground war. Primakov travelled to Baghdad, via Tehran, arriving on the night of 11 February. On the evening of the 11th, he met Saddam Hussein and the entire Iraqi leadership. Saddam was aggrieved by Soviet support for the "UN war against Iraq." Primakov reminded him that politics is the art of the possible and warned him that the United States would launch a crushing ground attack. In private, he put Gorbachev's proposals: Iraq should announce withdrawal of its troops from Kuwait in the shortest time possible and without condition.

Saddam did not reject the proposal but asked what guarantees would be given. In the early hours of the 13th, before Primakov's departure for Moscow, the Iraqis replied that they were "seriously studying the ideas...of the Soviet President" and would reply quickly. The result was Saddam's 15 February broadcast.

LEFT AND RIGHT: *MRLs and infantry stand poised along the border with Iraq and Kuwait awaiting the signal to go in.*

WHEN A TANK ISN'T A TANK

There are some strange looking vehicles massed along the Saudi-Kuwaiti border at the present time. They are the assault vehicles which use a tank chassis as a base for their own operational needs.

This may be bulldozing away Iraqi sand berms by strapping two metal blades on the front of the tank or, as in the case above, laying a bridge to span a wadi or ravine.

Tornado pilot clocks up 2,000 hours

Thirty-five-year-old Squadron Leader Gordon Buckley yesterday became the second RAF Tornado pilot to clock up 2,000 hours. He passed the landmark while on a daylight bombing mission against Iraq.

The Squadron Leader has also clocked up more than 1,000 hours in Jaguars and Hawks. The only other pilot to clock up 2,000 in a Tornado is Squadron Leader Gordon Reekie.

When Buckley returned to base his Squadron Chief, Wing Commander John Broadbent, presented him with a badge bearing the figure 2,000 in Arabic.

Day 31

Friday 15 February

At the UN Security Council meeting on the Gulf War, the British Ambassador, Sir David Hannay, insists the attacks on Iraq are in line with Council resolutions. He challenges the Iraqi ambassador, Abdul Amir al-Anbari, over the treatment of prisoners of war. Mr Anbari calls on the Security Council to condemn the slaughter in Iraq, and accuses the US of trying to destroy the country. The Soviet ambassador, Yuli Vorontsov, says Iraq is to blame for the hostilities. Both he and the Chinese Ambassador, Li Dao Yu, demand an intense effort to find a peaceful solution. In an interview with the BBC afterwards, Mr Anbari says that Iraq is willing to negotiate but its opponents refuse to do so.

King Hussein of Jordan says that he has probably failed in his friendship with President Bush because he could not persuade him that there might have been a way, other than war, to resolve the Gulf crisis.

German anti-aircraft missiles are transported by US aircraft to Turkey. German Defence Minister, Gerhard Stoltenberg, who is visiting Turkey, says the risk of an Iraqi attack on Turkey appears lower than at the start of the war.

Chancellor Kohl of Germany says the Iraqi proposal on withdrawal from Kuwait is unacceptable.

Flurry of last minute diplomacy

It has been announced that Iran will send a high level delegation to Iraq in the next few days. The message came from Iran's UN ambassador, Kamal Kharrazi, after hearing of Iraq's withdrawal offer from Kuwait. It was, he said, " a positive move".

Moscow's comments still appeared to be optimistic, in spite of President Bush's outright rejection of the proposals. It is widely thought that this is a ploy by Saddam Hussein to buy time for his forces.

US Defense Secretary, Dick Cheney, warned that there would be no pause in the war, but he did welcome Moscow's peace initiatives. He added that they must achieve Iraq's unconditional surrender; nothing less would be acceptable.

Casualty rate rises by the day

The wearing down of the Iraqi armed forces continues by the hour and by the day. Estimates of enemy casualties are now 50,000 dead.

The B-52s which are flying from England, Diego Garcia in the Indian Ocean, and from Spain, are continually pounding the Republican Guard positions with 20 tons of explosive from each plane as it passes over. The Guards are dug in north and west of Kuwait just inside the Iraqi border.

There is a shift, however, in the Allied campaign with a perceptible increase of missions by F-111s and AH-64 Apache helicopters attacking front-line troop positions. They are selecting points to attack with great accuracy and then strafing from the air, bombarding with artillery from MRLs and howitzers from the ground or using laser-guided bombs from the F-111s.

This, together with yesterday's announcement about withdrawal, has added significantly to the number of troops surrendering to the Allies. Leaflets are being dropped which tell the Iraqis how to give themselves up and what the escape route is.

Already the PoW camps, set well behind the Allied lines, are busy coping with a steady stream of men capitulating, often running directly through their own mine fields in an effort to surrender, rather than facing yet another round of Allied artillery or rocket fire.

Live firing exercises are on-going in the desert. There is no let-up from putting the pressure on Iraqi front-line positions.

"Old recipe in a new sauce"

British Air Chief Marshal Sir Patrick Hine, commented on Iraq's conditional withdrawal offer today by saying that it was "an old recipe in a new sauce". He saw no merit in the offer at all.

He went on to say that this notice of withdrawal would he thought be the first of many which would lead to an unconditional withdrawal by the forces in Kuwait.

Answering questions at the Riyadh briefing, he said, in response to the "targeting of Saddam" rumour of a few days previously, that it had never been an aim to kill Saddam Hussein or to bring him down.

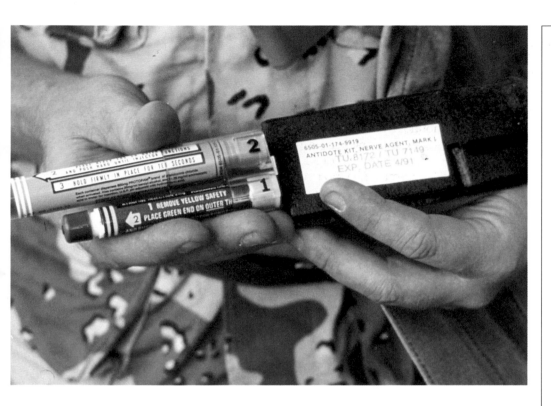

Saddam's ultimate weapon

An anti-chemical emergency injection kit has been issued to every member of Desert Storm. *There is a receding chance of chemicals being used but if they are, then the forces are prepared.*

The prospect of facing chemical weapons on the battlefield was taken very seriously during the run-up to the ground war. Iraq was known to have stocks of mustard gas, to be capable of producing it, and to be willing to use it in war - it had been used in the war against Iran.

More worrying still was the risk that Iraq might use nerve agents: Iraq was also known to be capable of producing the nerve gases Tabun and Sarin. Saddam Hussein had used Tabun against Kurds in the town of Halabja about three years before: and since these Kurds were mainly unarmed civilians and Iraqi citizens it seemed unlikely that he would be squeamish about using it against an armed enemy. What other chemicals he had was unknown - but there were fears that he might have something that was unknown.

Mustard gas is not a killer unless it is very concentrated. It causes burning and blistering of the skin and lungs, and temporary blindness. It disperses fairly slowly and contaminates ground for some time. Nerve agents work on the biochemistry of nerve endings, causing convulsions and death. They act fast - in a matter of minutes - but disperse and lose efficacy quickly.

Mustard gas and nerve agents are fearsome weapons against unprotected personnel: World War I and the grim photographs from Halabja provide adequate testimony. But pundits of the modern battlefield argue that they are not much of a weapon against properly equipped, well trained troops. Most of the Allied troops in the Gulf matched that description.

Gas masks and protection for the skin are sufficient against mustard gas, and Iraq's supplies were thought to be too small to last long if used in heavy concentration. Nerve agents require more thorough protection, but the chemical warfare protection outfits provided were well up to the job: uncomfortable, clumsy, difficult to wear for any length of time, but workable.

Day 32
Saturday 16 February

US military spokesman General Richard Neal says three more US aircraft have been lost.

A US military official in Saudi Arabia says that Allied artillery and helicopters are continuing attacks on Iraqi border positions and targeting areas where the Republican Guard are deployed.

The Iraqi authorities say that all bodies have now been recovered from the bombed air raid shelter, and that a total of 314 people were killed.

Foreign journalists in Iraq were taken to Fallujah, where bridges over the Euphrates were attacked last week by British Tornados and where two laser guided bombs accidently killed many civilians in the town's market. The British Ministry of Defence disputes some details of Iraq's account of the bombing.

Two Scud missiles are launched at Israel, but land in unpopulated areas. A total of 35 Scuds have now been fired at Israel since the war began.

Iran's Supreme National Council say it is now up to the Allies to respond to Iraq's conditional offer to withdraw from Kuwait and that coalition forces no longer have an excuse to continue their air raids on Iraq.

A MISERABLE ARMY

Glad to be in the hands of the enemy at last. After being pounded for nearly six weeks the Iraqi Army is giving up in droves. In several skirmishes today two US AH-64 Apache helicopters took 20 prisoners without the help of any ground support. A telling point to the commanders who are ever looking for signs of the enemy's weakness and lack of will to fight.

Day 33

Sunday 17 February

UNICEF send 50 tons of emergency medical supplies to Baghdad in a convoy travelling from Iran.

The International Confederation of Free Trade Unions alleges that Iraqi forces in Kuwait have arrested and tortured members of the country's trade union movement.

The Iranian news agency carries further reports of black rain falling in western parts of Iran from fires and explosions in Iraq. IRNA reports a resumption of heavy Allied bombing raids on southern Iraq.

The commander of British forces in the Gulf, Air Chief Marshal Sir Patrick Hine, says he thinks a ground offensive is now certain, and hopes that the ground campaign will be completed in a matter of weeks. He says the land battle will not begin until Iraq's combat effectiveness has been reduced to 50-60%, probably within two weeks.

The Iraqi ambassador to Paris, Abdul Razzak al-Hashimi, says that Iraq's conditional offer to withdraw from Kuwait is a clear indication that Saddam Hussein wants peace.

Baghdad Radio says yesterday's missile attack on Israel was aimed at the nuclear reactor at Dimona, and that they used their long-range Hijara missiles for the first time. The Israelis confirm that one missile landed in the Negev desert.

RISING TO THE CHALLENGE

Britain's Challenger tank provided the backbone of the Desert Rats' firepower in the Gulf. More than 150 of these 60-tonne machines were shipped over from Europe with spare parts. Powered by Rolls Royce engines the tanks were fitted with extra armour and a host of extras to enhance their fighting capability.

Armed with a 120 mm "fire on the move", the tanks are manned with a crew of four and organized into 11 squadrons split between the two British armoured brigades.

Challenger has never been tested in battle before and so far has acquitted itself flawlessly in conditions that are taking toll of even the most robust vehicles. In Europe the tank had gained a reputation for being unreliable, but not in the desert.

Day 34

Monday 18 February

The Commander of the multinational forces in the Gulf, General Norman Schwarzkopf, says the Allies will grant safe passage to the Iraqi Army if it begins withdrawing from Kuwait.

In the Gulf, assault ships, the USS *Tripoli* and guided missile cruiser USS *Princeton* are damaged by mines. Three Marines are injured aboard the USS *Princeton,* which is later withdrawn from duties for damage assessment. Allied minesweeping operations are extended into the northern Gulf.

A Soviet foreign ministry spokesman, Sergei Grigoriev, says that during his talks with Tariq Aziz, President Gorbachev put forward a new peace proposal. He says the plan also covers a spectrum of issues in the Gulf Region. The Soviet spokesman says that it involves a promise that Iraq will survive intact if it withdraws unconditionally from Kuwait. In a BBC interview, Mr Grigoriev says that the plan was drawn up bearing in mind that Saddam Hussein would need something to save face. Mr Aziz departs to deliver the plan to Saddam Hussein. A summary of the Soviet plan is sent to President Bush, but he is asked to keep the contents confidential. A copy of the plan is also delivered to British Prime Minister John Major.

Allied aircraft drop leaflets on cities in southern Iraq, urging residents to leave their homes to escape the bombing.

Bush rejects peace terms

According to Baghdad Radio, President Bush rejected the Soviet peace plan outright. In fact, the American response was less categorical than has been painted by the Iraqis.

Not surprisingly, since the plan addressed only the question of immediate withdrawal, President Bush said that "it fell well short of what was required". In particular, the United States was concerned about possible guarantees to Saddam Hussein about his political future and the implications of the plan for the issues of "linkage" to the Palestinian Question. Additionally, the Americans wanted a detailed timetable of withdrawal which would include the Iraqi Army's abandonment, where it stood, of all tanks and armour.

Nevertheless it was acknowledged in Washington that the plan meant that peace hopes were "alive", but only if the specific details for withdrawal were made firm.

At the same time, it was made clear that the clock was running on for the land invasion, with the US giving the Soviets 36 hours to persuade the Iraqis to pull out of Kuwait.

Ministers in London did not hold out much hope, either, that the Soviets could persuade the Iraqis to withdraw.

Iraq is doctoring war damage, says Pentagon

In a briefing by the Pentagon yesterday the US produced photographic evidence that purported to show that Iraq was trying to dupe the world to gain sympathy for its civilian casualties.

It showed that an Allied bomb had missed its target and exploded over 100 yards away from a mosque. When the same site was photographed the following day the dome of the mosque was entirely missing.

BELOW: *Not only was there darkness and gloom in Moscow but also in Kuwait as the oil fires from the burning well-heads caused a gigantic cloud of oily smoke which hung in the skies of the city and hinterland.*

BELOW: *PoWs being herded into lines prior to being transported back to holding areas well away from the battle front.*

GULF NOSE ART

Intriguing things appeared during the Gulf War on the sides of aircraft. These were not the high-tech arrays of weaponry that one would normally expect, but a human and creative "art-form" that has its roots in the planes of World War II and the Korean War. During the days of the cold-war peace, any painting of images on aircraft to personalize them was looked down upon and in the end forbidden by official order. With the advent of the Gulf War, however, many aircraft from both the US and RAF suddenly sprouted images, usually in colour and often as not raunchy in nature, on the sides of its fighters, bombers and transport craft. Pictured above is "The Boss", a British Jaguar, which also sports an amazing array of mission marks recording the aircraft's exploits, ranging from bombing to photo-reconaissance.

Heavy pounding goes on and on

As part of the last-minute preparations, in the last two days British and US troops have attacked Iraqi positions just across the Saudi-Kuwait border. Both tanks and artillery have been shelling Iraqi positions, supplementing the air bombardments, but so far there has been no response. In the first engagement by British soldiers against Iraqi positions, self-propelled guns and MLRs (multiple launch rocket systems) advanced to the border of Saudi Arabia and Kuwait and fired on 18 targets. Some troops have also crossed into Kuwait and bulldozed routes through the berm that marks the border. Meanwhile, coalition forces have been conducting a mine-clearing operation in the Gulf. Minesweepers have found 22 mines in the northern Gulf so far.

Day 35

Tuesday 19 February

White House spokesman Marlin Fitzwater says he has seen nothing in the Soviet peace plan so far to change the course of the war. He denies that the Kremlin asked Washington to hold off any ground operations while Soviet diplomacy took place.

Allied aircraft resumed bombing raids on Baghdad - the first big attacks since the raid on the bunker that claimed so many civilian lives.

A senior US Army officer says that plans have been drawn up for installing temporary governments in areas of Iraq and Kuwait that fall into Allied hands.

Pope John Paul II asks Roman Catholic leaders from around the world involved in the war to meet him at the Vatican on 4-5 March 1991.

Iran's Foreign Minister, Ali Akbar Velayati, says he is satisfied from the discussions with his Iraqi counterparts that Iraq has agreed to withdraw from Kuwait without preconditions. He calls for the multinational forces to respond with a 48-hour ceasefire and plans for a timetable for withdrawal.

The director of the Iraqi Red Crescent Society appeals for more international medical and food aid, and for exports to help combat water shortages. In Geneva, the Red Cross says it believes epidemics such as cholera could break out.

SCALP HUNTER

Everyone is waiting to see how the Apache behaves in battle. This multimillion dollar helicopter is "state-of-the-art", and like much other equipment in the Kuwaiti war theatre has never been tested in combat. The AH-64 is the US Army's main battlefield helicopter specializing in anti-tank warfare. It is also used to support ground troops.

It is incredibly agile for its size and it has a rate of climb of over 3,000 feet a minute, but it is vulnerable to ground fire from small arms and in *Desert Shield* has been plagued with electrical malfunctions on its elaborate computer systems. Production and maintenance problems have not helped either.

But once airborne and out hunting, either in packs or with just a "buddy", this helicopter is likely to prove itself tenfold. Last week 41 Iraqis surrendered just at the sight of two machines flying in towards them and another time AH-64s helped destroy a bunker and claim over 400 PoWs.

Its weapons platform can pack an ominous punch, with a pair of quad-loaded Hellfire missiles slung under it as well as two 70mm rocket pods on the twin booms extending from its fuselage. To give just that little extra, it has a 30mm chain-gun which can fire off some 1,200 rounds of ammunition.

Day 36

Wednesday 20 February

Iraq's deputy Prime Minister, Saadoun Hammadi, who was at the Moscow talks with Tariq Aziz, arrives directly in Peking for talks with the Chinese Prime Minister, Li Peng, who urges an immediate and unconditional Iraqi withdrawal.

The joint commander of the Allied Forces, General Norman Schwarzkopf, says he believes the Iraqi military machine is on the verge of collapse. In response, the Iraqi Information Minister, Latif Nassif Jasim, accuses General Schwarzkopf of quoting "lies and fantasies".

State Department officials in Washington say the US is to make big cuts in aid to Tunisia because of its stance over the Gulf War.

Italian Prime Minister, Giulio Andreotti, comes out in broad support of the Soviet peace plan.

Further steps are to be taken to protect Saudi Arabia's main desalination plant at Jubail from the huge oil slick moving south down the coast from Kuwait. The Saudis say they have extracted 100,000 barrels of oil from the slick, and more protective booms are being moved in to shield the complex, which provides Riyadh with most of its drinking water.

Saddam must decide today - is it peace or a ground war?

Saddam Hussein is playing for time. This is the only possible conclusion that anyone can come to.

After delivering his 35 minute tirade against the Allies news came that Saddam would reply to the Moscow peace proposals "soon" and that Tarik Aziz, the Foreign Minister would visit Moscow with an answer. It soon became clear however that Tariq Aziz was powerless to negotiate and that any advances made between the two powers would have to be ratified in Baghdad.

Moscow in its turn said that it was looking for a clear, prompt and un-ambiguous answer; however, there was no deadline.

In Paris though, M Roland Dumas said that there was a 24 hour deadline to the reply otherwise there would be a full-scale attack - that deadline was already 12 hours shorter. Both London and Washington later denied that this was the case, and in Russia Mr Vitaly Churkin, a Soviet Foreign Ministry spokesman said that "it was a very complicated issue".

Saddened by the news that Washington had dismissed the Soviet peace offer, he strongly denied that there was a rift between the two superpowers.

"We do not think Mr Bush's statement is a rejection of the plan...We have continued to exchange views with Washington. It is a normal process."

In Washington the rejection of the peace proposals was countered by President Bush, who demanded that his own set of proposals be observed by Saddam.

The terms, which gave little or no face-saving formula to Saddam, were: the recognition of the al-Sabah family by Iraq as legitimate rulers of that country; the acceptance of a Kuwaiti population list as valid; immediate repatriation of all Allied prisoners of war; the instant withdrawal of all Iraqi forces without armour or chemical weapons. The Allies told Moscow that the terms of their agreement should be spelled out and "signed in big large letters with Saddam Hussein's name so there is no mistake".

BREAKING THE BARRIER

To invade Kuwait the Allies must make a frontal assault on the Iraqi border defences. These stretch the entire length of Kuwait's southern border, round the coast as far north as the Iranian border.

Throughout January and even now the Allies have been giving close attention to these fortifications and have been attempting to breach them and destroy them. It is on this layering of forts "in-depth" that Saddam is pinning his hopes of winning a land war. It was through this defensive tactic that he was so successful in his war against Iran.

Assuming that he has some artillery left after the opening phase of the ground war, the Allied troops will have to deploy through a series of channels which are directed into specific areas where Iraqi artillery is pointed. These are known as "killing grounds", where the enemy artillery is able to pick off Allied vehicles and create bottlenecks so that even more fire power can be called in. This is why it is so important to destroy as much as possible of the enemy ground forces.

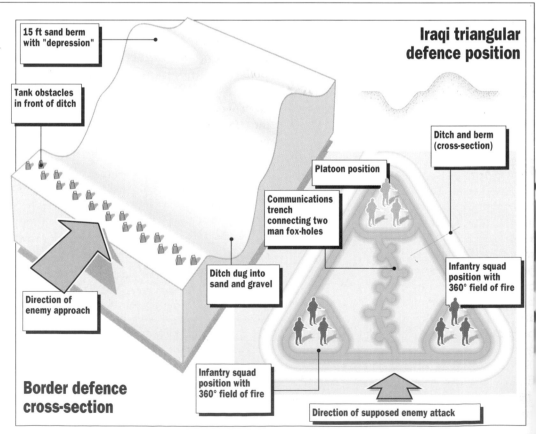

15 ft sand berm with "depression"

Iraqi triangular defence position

Tank obstacles in front of ditch

Ditch and berm (cross-section)

Platoon position

Communications trench connecting two man fox-holes

Infantry squad position with 360° field of fire

Ditch dug into sand and gravel

Direction of enemy approach

Border defence cross-section

Infantry squad position with 360° field of fire

Direction of supposed enemy attack

Three ground battles in 24 hours. Invasion preparations go ahead

Yesterday was a day for an Army aviation man to remember - in one of three ground actions over 500 prisoners were taken when AH-64s and OH-58s swooped on a bunker system north of the Saudi-Iraqi border. During the action, in which the bunkers were subjected to heavy rocket attacks by the helicopters, up to 15 bunkers were destroyed and 500 Iraqis gave themselves up.

No estimates were given of the casualty figures but this is a clear indication that the consistent bombardment and attacks are now lowering morale significantly.

Mass flights of these AH-64 Apache helicopters are now a common sight to both Allied and Iraqi ground troops.

Such were the numbers surrendering that the US flew in Chinook helicopters and personnel into the area to ferry back the PoWs.

Another battle was later described as an "encounter engagement" which took place on the border, if anyone really knows where that is now. In the battle, five Iraqi tanks were destroyed along with 20 pieces of artillery.

The third engagement happened much further east along the Saudi-Kuwaiti border and involved pan-Arab forces from Syria, Kuwait and Egypt as well as elements of the Saudi national forces.

A Saudi military spokesman described it as a "very large air and artillery bombardment" during which eight tanks, two observation buildings and three vehicles were destroyed.

Day 37

Thursday 21 February

The Arab Committee for Medical Assistance to Iraq says dozens of Arab doctors and tons of medical supplies have arrived in Amman en route to Iraq in the past two days.

A Pentagon spokesman, General Thomas Kelly, says a ground offensive to oust the Iraqis from Kuwait will not be easy for the US and its Allies.

In a broadcast over Baghdad Radio, Saddam Hussein condemns Arab governments opposed to Iraq as traitors to their people, mentioning in particular President Mubarak and King Fahd of Saudi Arabia. In a 35-minute speech he gives no indication whether or not Iraq is prepared to accept the Soviet peace plan. The US expresses disappointment in the speech, and White House spokesman Marlin Fitzwater says the war to liberate Kuwait will continue.

The British Army, in conjunction with US forces, unleashes its heaviest onslaught yet on Iraqi positions in Kuwait.

The exiled Kuwaiti Finance Minister, Sheikh Ali al–Khalifa al-Sabah, repeats Kuwait's demand for full reparations from Iraq once the Gulf conflict is over. He says that once the legitimate government is returned to power it may impose martial law for a short period, but there will be a return to the 1962 constitution and new parliamentary elections.

Saddam says "yes" to Soviet plan!

At the eleventh hour Saddam Hussein has agreed to the Soviet plan for peace and will withdraw from Kuwait. This is how the timetable of events unfolded.

Gorbachev met Aziz as soon as the latter reached the Kremlin. Through the night they talked, outlining areas of agreement. Iraq agreed to accept Resolution 660, but would not meet the proposed deadline for withdrawal. Gorbachev insisted that "the proposed deadline can and must be reduced to a minimum." At 3:30 a.m. a press spokesman announced that agreement had been reached and that the details were being worked out. Gorbachev rang Bush, who was sceptical and concerned about coalition PoWs. He thought it impossible to ignore the damage inflicted on Kuwait. Bessmertnykh and Primakov were warned to pay close heed to Bush's concerns.

The talks resumed at the Foreign Ministry, the Iraqis clearly stalling. It took an hour to deal with the question of PoWs and in the end the Russians had to insist they be released within three days of a ceasefire.

The Iraqis wanted six weeks to withdraw from Kuwait, taking their time until the season of sandstorms would have made military operations very difficult. The Russians attempted to split the issue, making withdrawal from Kuwait City the priority, to be accomplished in four days, and allowing twenty-one days for the remainder of the country. No agreement was possible on sanctions and reparation payments to Kuwait. Aziz had instructions not to budge on this issue.

As Aziz did not have the power to conclude an agreement, he wanted Primakov to fly there with him to meet Saddam. Meantime, Bush had issued an ultimatum giving the Iraqis until 1700 GMT on the 23rd to begin their withdrawal, which would have to be complete within one week.

Tariq Aziz was urged to ring Baghdad as time was running out. Again the Iraqis seem to be stalling. The Allies are not.

A Kuwaiti soldier in a patriotic pose.

"We have broadened the frontier"

The US would not be drawn on whether the land offensive had started, but they did agree that there had been "forays" into enemy territory and it is perfectly clear to anyone visiting the front-line that the "softening up is going apace". "We are broadening the frontier" was the closest anyone could get to an answer.

What is anyone gaining from this game of cat-and-mouse? Allied guns move up to the firing position, range, shoot and move away, while the Iraqis sit there and await the next barrage.

Iraq has more artillery than the Allies, and it can shell further than any Allied weapon. However, they are static, as Saddam has chosen to fight from dug-in fortifications which, once the Allies have spotted them on their radar, are vulnerable to both air and ground attack.

The Allies claim to have knocked out about one-third of Iraq's artillery, but this leaves over 850 pieces in Kuwait alone. Allied firepower is rated at just over 1,600 pieces; it is mobile and uses fewer types of ammunition.

Against this the Iraqis have deployed the G-5 gun, made by the late Gerald Bull of "supergun " fame, which is capable of firing a shell five miles further than any of the Allied weapons.

Like the Allies, Iraq has Multiple Rocket Launchers, but mainly of a much earlier vintage. On both sides the "shoot and scoot" principle will be used.

Self-propelled guns are again ranged on each side but the Allies have an edge with more modern howitzers like the M109A2 and M110A2, the first having a range of 12 miles and the latter up to 19 miles.

In the end it will boil down to whether it is strategically better to absorb blows from well dug and planned fortifications such as the Iraqis have chosen to build, or to be mobile and able to respond in a quick and varied manner, depending on the scenario being played out in front of you. Only time will tell.

US Secretary of State, James Baker, discusses the Soviet peace plan in phone conversations with foreign ministers of several coalition partners, including Britain, France and Egypt.

A Saudi military spokesman says Iraq fired a Scud missile towards Bahrain during the night. It was hit by a Patriot missile and its debris fell into the sea.

The commander of a battalion of US helicopters in Saudi Arabia is relieved of his post after an incident on 17 February in which he mistakenly fired on two friendly American armoured vehicles, killing two soldiers. Lt-Col. Ralph Hayes is said to have violated rules forbidding commanding officers from personally engaging enemy forces.

A French Foreign Ministry statement says the Soviet peace plan is a step in the right direction, but several points remain unclear and that the Iraqi withdrawal must be immediate and rapid.

Baghdad Radio makes only an oblique reference to the Moscow talks, speaking of Iraq's "deep belief in peace and the initiative of friends".

Officials at the UN Environmental Programme say that the oil slick which spilled into the northern Gulf from Kuwait last month may contain only one tenth of the oil that was originally suggested.

Deadline goes unheeded despite international peace moves

There was little time left as Saturda dawned in Baghdad; all the world wa holding its breath, waiting for a positiv response.

In Moscow, a senior Soviet diploma was confident: "As soon as Saddar Hussein agrees to the plan, the war i over."

The new propositions were hammere out in a hectic session only hour previously and transmitted to Baghdad fo instant approval. In brief, the term appeared to give a guaranteed timetabl for the unconditional withdrawal of Iraq troops once the ceasefire begins. Iraq would withdraw from Kuwait City fou days after the the start of the ceasefire an from all of Kuwait within 21 days. Afte that the UN resolutions governin sanctions would be lifted.

"But these terms have not been agree by President Hussein", said Mr Vital Ignatenko, "and fall short of Presiden Bush's ultimatum."

At 2:00 a.m. the Russians receive Saddam's agreement to the withdrawa plan. At midday, Aziz announced i Moscow that Iraq had agreed to a immediate and unconditional withdrawa Aziz then boarded a flight to Baghdad.

Gorbachev immediately contacted a the countries of the Security Council speaking to Bush for 75 minutes. Th Russians were convinced that th differences between the two withdrawa plans could be reconciled. There were n further contacts with Baghdad.

A Russian spokesman made clear th Soviet sorrow that "the world could no resolve this by peaceful means" addin that he believed "Iraq still has time to ac but unfortunately it is not days or months but hours and minutes."

Military ready to go now

There is now no doubt that the Allied forces are more than ready to go into action and are waiting for the code word to go. Orders have been circulated and engines of tanks and other AFVs are being warmed up and checked over and over again.

Final practice is taking place (*see both pictures*), so no hitch will occur. Reports from Northern Saudi Arabia on the Iraqi border say that US troops are actively preparing for the ground assault by breaching the border sand berms, clearing minefields and tank obstacles and constructing fuelling points. There are some indications that FARPs (Forward Air Refuelling Points) have been established only yesterday inside Iraq. One combat engineer was quoted as saying he had cleared gateways all along the borders.

At sea a huge force of 18,000 US Marines is waiting to go in. For the past few days the bombardment of the coast from the "big ships" *Missouri* and *Wisconsin* has intensified, and there has been a heavy increase in minesweeping activity by both the British Navy and other coalition forces.

In the air, the same relentless pressure goes on. Observers speak of watching sticks of bombs from B-52s strike Iraqi positions far on the horizon, feel the bombs' impact and watch smoke clouds sometimes over five miles across filling the air.

After some days of poor weather, the RAF have been able to mount more missions over Kuwait and Iraq; three "smart bomb" attacks over Iraq were balanced by Jaguars carrying out three sorties against command and control centres in Kuwait itself.

Flying low is very difficult for the US A-10s as visibility is now obscured by low clouds, smoke from bombing as well as smoke billowing from the well-heads that Iraq has destroyed. The latest estimate is that over 180 are on fire, and the number is increasing daily.

Day 39

Saturday 23 February

The Soviet Middle East envoy, Yevgeny Primakov, speaking on American television, says it should be possible to resolve the situation within a day or two, unless a military action develops further. He says that Saddam Hussein agreed on 22 February - through the Soviet embassy in Baghdad - that he would withdraw his troops without conditions.

The Kuwaiti ambassador to the UN, Mohammed Abulhasan, tells the Security Council that at least 28,000 Kuwaiti nationals are now missing and that many of them have been taken by force to Iraq. In addition, he says that there are also more than 8,000 Kuwaiti prisoners of war - more than half the strength of Kuwait's army.

Turkey's President Ozal says he believes the Gulf War will bring a wave of democratic change to the Middle East like the one that has already swept through Eastern Europe. He denies suggestions that Turkey has joined the anti-Iraq coalition in order to grab something for itself, and his forces will not take part in any ground assault.

A US military spokesman in Saudi Arabia, General Richard Neal, says he has no information that the Iraqis are pulling out of Kuwait , but there are reports of atrocities against civilians. He says the number of Allied air sorties over Kuwait has reached a new record in the last 24 hours.

GO, GO, GO!

Just as dawn began to light the desert, the first waves of the ground attack commenced. After a terrifying bombardment by artillery, and while the Iraqis were still stunned by the ferocity of the onslaught, the tanks went in, smashing through enemy defences "like a knife through butter". On the entire front the picture was similar with virtually no resistance to the initial wave.

They were 15 miles into enemy territory before the troops actually took any prisoners. When they did surrender, they were smiling and glad that the ordeal was over.

Day 40

Sunday 24 February

At 0100 GMT (0400 local time), the Allied ground offensive is launched against Iraq.

Several US TV networks report that a large number of Iraqi front line troops are surrendering.

President Bush goes on television to announce that he has told his commanders in the Gulf to use all the forces available to them to eject Iraqi units from Kuwait. He says the ultimatum delivered on 22 February 1991, was the last chance for Saddam Hussein to withdraw, but instead the Iraqi leader had chosen to redouble his efforts to destroy Kuwait and its people.

In the first full military briefing of the ground campaign, General Schwarzkopf says the Allies have achieved all their first day objectives. He says the whole Allied force is involved in the operation. 5,500 Iraqi prisoners have been captured in the first ten hours of the operation, and he says the offensive is proceeding with dramatic success. General Schwarzkopf goes on to say that US, British, Saudi and Kuwaiti naval forces are conducting full missions - including amphibious assaults - along the Kuwaiti coast. He says Allied casualties have been remarkably light and that there has been no sign of chemical weapons being used.

Iraqi forces left stunned as ground troops rush onwards un-checked

On the second day of the war the Allies are continuing their advance on a broad front - some 300 miles long - stretching in an arc from the Gulf coast deep into Iraq, with hundreds of thousands of troops sweeping through the desert.

There are four main "arms" to the advance. On the extreme left is XVIII Corps and US 101st Airborne Division, with the French 6th Daguet Division, leap-frogging deep inside Iraq. Next to it is the VII Corps, which includes 1st British Armoured Division. Inside Kuwait is a mixed force of US Marines and Arab forces, including Egyptian, Saudi and Kuwaiti, which has punched a hole through the Iraqi defences and is closing on Kuwait City. And on the extreme right US Marines and Arab forces are pushing up the coast.

The berms which were supposed to incinerate the advancing troops, were never set alight in the end. Presumably the Iraqis just didn't have time to fire them before they retreated.

There is more resistance than on the first day, when the Allies simply over-ran Saddam's miserable little conscript army eager to surrender. Now the Allies are meeting better-trained forces, and have come up against the much-discussed Republican Guard for the first time. But casualties are still very light.

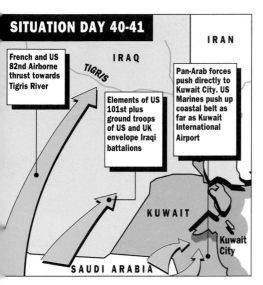

SITUATION DAY 40-41

IRAN

IRAQ

TIGRIS

French and US 82nd Airborne thrust towards Tigris River

Elements of US 101st plus ground troops of US and UK envelope Iraqi battalions

Pan-Arab forces push directly to Kuwait City. US Marines push up coastal belt as far as Kuwait International Airport

KUWAIT

Kuwait City

SAUDI ARABIA

Tank battles against Guards

Two large-scale tank battles were reported, one in southern Iraq near the Kuwaiti border, and one about 40 miles south of Kuwait City. In the second tank battle Saudi and Kuwaiti forces, supported by US Marines with M60 tanks, destroyed 50-60 Iraqi tanks. By the end of the day, the Allies claimed in all to have destroyed more than 270 Iraqi tanks and to have captured more than 20,000 prisoners, many of whom are being marshalled back behind the advancing lines with helicopters (*see picture below*).

Saudi and Kuwaiti troops poised to enter Kuwait City

By the end of the second day of the ground war the Allied troops (including Kuwaitis and Saudis) had halted some 40 miles south of Kuwait City, half an hour's drive before the war. They were now poised to retake the city.

The Allies had punched through the Iraqi front line without any trouble, and the much-vaunted berms (sand walls, with ditches behind them which are filled with oil) had never been set alight. The landscape seemed empty of people, except for troops anxious to surrender, and the desert highway to the city was littered with abandoned and burned-out vehicles and tanks.

The pan-Arab force has been given a difficult job of pushing up through the worst of the Iraqi fortifications. On their eastern flank they were supported by the US Marine Corps who advanced up the coast, in the process beating off a strong counter-attack. They are now fighting for control of Kuwait City International Airport.

Day 41
Monday 25 February

In a message to mark his country's National Day, the Emir of Kuwait, Sheikh Jabir-al-Ahmed al-Sabah, says he prays for a speedy victory in the war, and urges Kuwaitis to unite to rebuild their country.

The US Defense Department says only a dozen or so American troops have been killed in the first few hours of the ground offensive.

An Iraqi Silkworm missile is fired at British and American ships off the coast of Kuwait, but is intercepted and destroyed by missiles from HMS *Gloucester*.

An Iraqi military communique (no. 62) says their 3rd Brigade has launched an all-out offensive, and that the enemy has been forced to retreat after an eight-hour battle.

The commander of French forces in the Gulf, General Michel Roquejeoffre, says his troops have neutralized an entire Iraqi division, and have penetrated 160 km into Iraq.

Baghdad Radio reports that Saddam Hussein has ordered his forces to withdraw from Kuwait to positions they occupied on 1 August 1990. The broadcast says the order to withdraw has been taken in accordance with the Soviet peace proposal, which the Allies rejected before the start of the ground offensive.

"Kuwait is liberated
enter City to tremer

- troops
ous welcome

On 26 February Kuwait City was abandoned by the Iraqis, after Saddam Hussein's order to the troops to withdraw immediately from Kuwait.

The US Army and Arab troops and tanks enmeshed the city while Iraqi forces fled north in disarray, having been deserted by their officers. Allied commanders attacked, taking many prisoners in the process.

The Iraqi forces were fleeing on the main highway "bumper to bumper" and were bombed frenetically by the US Air Force. In fact there were so many US jets converging on the escape route that there were fears of mid-air collisions.

It had been made clear by the White House that Iraqis would be safe only if they abandoned weapons and armoured vehicles, while the British Prime Minister, John Major, told the House of Commons: "I do not believe that our troops or world public opinion would forgive us if at this stage we permitted the Iraqis to withdraw with their weapons."

US Marines entered Kuwait City and occupied the US Embassy. Bob McKeown of CBS News made the first broadcast from the city. He said the Emir's palace had been destroyed and streets were "deserted, hulks of automobiles strewn about, and very, very few people on the streets". McKeown confirmed reports of executions, rape and torture in the city during the last few days of Iraqi occupation, and told the BBC: "Everyone had a story about a friend or relative who had been killed."

Day 42
Tuesday 26 February

The Kuwaiti government-in-exile says it will not accept any action which amounts to less than a complete and unconditional withdrawal, together with the restoration of Kuwait's legitimate government in accordance with UN resolutions. The statement says the Iraqi regime has a long history of lying and is not to be trusted.

The UN Security Council met in closed session at the request of the Soviet Union. Iraq's representative at the United Nations, Abdul Amir al-Anbari, says that Iraqi troops have already begun to withdraw from Kuwait, in compliance with Resolution 660, and that a ceasefire should be in place to ensure that they can pull out in safety. He says that Iraq feels that all other UN Security Council resolutions have been superseded. Western delegations reject this, saying Baghdad should implement all the relevant UN resolutions.

White House spokesman Marlin Fitzwater makes a statement saying the war against Iraq will continue. Speaking after a meeting between President Bush and his top security advisers, Mr Fitzwater says they have heard nothing to alter their position. He says that coalition forces will not attack soldiers in retreat, if they are not armed, but if they move as a combat unit they would still be subject to the rules of war.

Iraqi withdrawal turns into a rout on Mutla Ridge

The retreat from Kuwait to Basra is Iraq's biggest defeat. One newspaper has described it as Iraq's Dunkirk, as it turned from a withdrawal, to a rout, to a massacre.

It happened last night as Iraqi troops, desperate to escape any further Allied attacks, fled up the highway from Kuwait to Basra on whatever vehicles they could commandeer - luxury limousines, fire engines, police cars, tanks, trucks and bulldozers.

But they never reached Basra. US aircraft, alerted to the retreat, attacked the convoy with cluster bombs and rockets, returning again and again to bomb the sitting target. Pilots are said to have described it as a "turkey shoot", and compared the attack to "shooting fish in a barrel". Stuck bumper to bumper, the convoy ground to a halt in an impassable, four-mile-long traffic jam where it was bombed into annihilation.

Afterwards, the scene was one of indescribable carnage. The route was lined with thousands of burned-out and abandoned vehicles. Many had been stuffed full of loot which spilled out onto the highway - carpets, jewellery, toys, cosmetics, video sets - anything the fleeing soldiers could lay their hands on in their last panic-stricken hours.

Corpses lay in and out of the burned-out vehicles, many charred beyond all possibility of identification. It was a scene many Allied soldiers will never forget.

Mopping-up operations continue

In spite of the total capitulation of the forces in Kuwait City, a number of isolated incidents are occurring with Iraqi sharpshooters, usually Republican Guards, putting up spirited resistance. It has been announced that after two days of stiff fighting the International Airport in Kuwait City has been freed of remaining enemy soldiers. The large quantities of live ammunition littering the terrain is causing some concern.

ABOVE: *The carnage of Mutla Ridge where the "turkey shoot" took place will remain engraved on everyone's memory for years to come.*
LEFT: *Regardless of what happened at Mutla there was still euphoria at having ended the war so quickly. In just 100 hours the Iraqi Army had been annihilated inside Kuwait.*

Day 43

Wednesday 27 February

The commander of the Allied forces in the Gulf, General Norman Schwarzkopf, says that the gates are now closed on the Iraqi forces still in the war zone and there is no way out for them. Speaking at a news briefing in Saudi Arabia, General Schwarzkopf says the Allied casualties have been almost miraculously light. He adds that during the ground offensive, coalition forces were in a position where there was nothing between them and Baghdad. He says that if it were the intention of the Allies to take Iraq, they could have done so then unopposed.

The UN Security Council begins meeting to discuss Iraq's announcement that it is prepared to comply with more of the Council's resolutions on the Gulf War.

British Prime Minister John Major and US President Bush agree by telephone on the suspension of Gulf hostilities.

At the end of a closed session the UN Security Council calls on Iraq to make a clear commitment to comply with all Security Council resolutions relating to the Kuwaiti situation in order to bring about a ceasefire. It also demands an Iraqi undertaking to release all prisoners of war and all Kuwaiti nationals.

The War is over - official. Bush suspends all ops

One hundred hours after the ground war began, President Bush announced the end of hostilities. As Allied forces reported further sweeping victories, penetrating deep into Iraq, Bush declared "Kuwait is liberated", that Iraq had been defeated and that the Allies' objectives had been met.

He also said the ceasefire was dependent on Iraqi agreement not to attack coalition forces, or to continue Scud missile attacks - otherwise the war would continue. All PoWs had to be released, together with Kuwaitis taken as hostages as Iraqis fled from Kuwait.

The statement came after a ceasefire appeal from Baghdad had earlier been rejected by the White House, and when the Allied forces were on the brink of a conclusive victory.

The US Secretary of State, James Baker, will fly to the Middle East next week to begin the negotiation of a post-war settlement. There have been hints recently that Washington hoped that the army and people of Iraq would turn against Saddam and overthrow him. King Fahd of Saudi Arabia also indicated that he would drop demands for reparations if Saddam Hussein is overthrown.

There was no immediate reaction from Baghdad, but the UN Security Council might reconvene to hear the possible Iraqi response.

A military briefing in Riyadh took place later that day and gave an indication of the overwhelming scale of the victory. 42 Iraqi army divisions which had been deployed in Kuwait or Southern Iraq had been destroyed or rendered completely ineffective, with the surviving two divisions scattered across the battlefield.

Kuwait City is free, but at what price?

The horror that has been in Kuwait is beginning to emerge. The city itself looks like pictures of Hell, as a thick pall of smoke from burning oil wells hangs over the ruined city. In the streets reporters are bombarded with people, all with horrendous stories to tell of rape, torture and murder. 5,000 men are reported to have been abducted in the last few hours before the Iraqi retreat. Young men - or any man or boy between the ages of 15 and 45 - had simply been stopped in the street and loaded into army buses. No one doubts that they may never be seen again.

The destruction has been total, and deliberate. The National Museum, its treasures long since looted, was set on fire. The National Library was also burned, and the parliament building was gutted and then bombarded by tanks. All major hotels were torched and shops looted.

Day 44

Thursday 28 February

The UN Secretary General, Javier Pérez de Cuéllar, says he is ready to send UN peacekeeping forces to monitor a ceasefire, and that a senior UN official consulted at least 20 nations to see which would send observers to the Gulf.

The Iraqi ambassador to the UN, Abdul Amir al-Anbari, conveys his country's acceptance of all twelve UN resolutions to the Secretary General, Javier Pérez de Cuéllar.

In Baghdad, despite the lack of any official Iraqi announcement, the end of the war is celebrated by soldiers firing thousands of rounds into the air.

FTERMATH

WHETHER or not war changes anything is a question which historians are fond of debating. It seems that while the structures of international politics are clearly altered - by the two World Wars, for example - it is sometimes difficult to detect domestic changes, certainly within the victor states. So soon after the war in the Gulf, and its immediate aftermath, it is still difficult to draw any firm conclusions about the consequences.

Some things seem clearer than others: that there was great popular dissatisfaction with the Iraqi government perhaps came as no surprise; that the al-Sabahs were equally disliked by many Kuwaitis was news to many, including journalists who reported on the situation in Kuwait after the ceasefire.

The effect on Kuwait

Kuwaitis and others who endured Iraq's occupation, suffered privation, humiliation, and in some cases, death. After the initial jubilation of liberation, they became increasingly dissatisfied and angry as their endurance was tested with yet more privation, humiliation and death, this time at the hands of their own army, police and government. During the period of occupation, many Kuwaitis engaged in resistance; many more became part of community networks which in effect administered districts, including making provision for foreigners in hiding, or Kuwaitis who were vulnerable to the Iraqis. Thus the adversity of war gave rise to new and more democratic structures which also crossed national and cultural boundaries. (This included the 170,000 Palestinians who had remained in Kuwait, out of approximately half a million who had

West Bank Palestinians weep at the news that Saddam Hussein's troops have withdrawn from Kuwait and have been routed.

lived there before the crisis.)

Kuwait's rulers, on the other hand, had fled, taking up residence in a luxury hotel in the Saudi resort of Taif. With the ceasefire it became clear that the Kuwait government-in-exile had made no plans for the relief of the city. In fact, residents found themselves less well provisioned than they had been under the Iraqis. Kuwaiti security forces arrived and

"I'm not going to change another thing..."

GENERAL NORMAN SCHWARZKOPF

immediately began a reign of terror, directed primarily against Palestinians. In the meantime, the garbage remained on the streets, and there was little food or water. There was also no electricity, despite the fact that a contract was awarded for the repair of the chandeliers in the Emir's palace. The government's priority was to restore *business* as usual; urgently needed food did not move until the value of the Kuwaiti dinar had been fixed against the Saudi riyal. Only belatedly was it realized that the population might require humanitarian aid.

At a political level there were tensions. The resistance movement survived as a number of significant political organizations, mainly secular democratic or Shi'ite fundamentalist. They have made demands for rapid progress towards democracy, in the first instance the restoration of the 1962 constitution and free elections to the assembly. But the al-Sabahs, while publicly accepting the restoration of constitutional government, have failed to commit themselves to any timetable, saying only that there are more important tasks of reconstruction to be dealt with first.

There is thus a division within the Kuwaiti community between those who stayed and those who fled into exile. It is perhaps significant that there is a reservoir of discontent among non-civil service professionals and army officers returning from captivity in Iraq. Both are

After the war came the suffering. Kurds fled in hundreds of thousands into the mountains between Iraq and Turkey.

highly critical of the government's competence during the crisis and its aftermath. In particular, captured officers point to the failure to offer any real resistance to the invading Iraqis, with the army simply being sacrificed. This is a potentially explosive combination which, should it ignite, could push Kuwait in the direction of either democracy or military dictatorship.

At the same time, there are persistent, and probably accurate, rumours that some members of the ruling family and its ministerial retainers are behind the death squads which are stirring up anti-Palestinian, anti-foreign and anti-democratic resentment. It is doubtful whether the Kuwaitis alone possess either the manpower or the skills required to reconstruct and operate the *ante bellum* economy. Moreover, the terror has persuaded many Kuwaiti-born Palestinian professionals to leave the country in disgust, preferring the West Bank to what

has taken place in Kuwait.

What seems clear is that the war has exposed all the incompetence of the Kuwaiti autocracy which now - like the Bourbons in 1789 or the Romanovs in 1917 - totters under its own weight, dependent on foreign labour yet fearful of it, and temporarily short of cash. Thus weakened, the Crown Prince's government has resigned, though no formula has yet been found which will satisfy the opposition and enable a replacement to take its place. The al-Sabahs must be hoping that in time they will be able to buy their way out of their difficulties.

Aftermath in Iraq

Iraq's defeat immediately plunged the country into a civil war which threatened

....

Will Saddam's promises to the Kurds ever be fulfilled? Only time will tell. In the meantime fear is ever present.

to tear it to pieces as two constituent parts, the Shias in the south and the Kurds in the north, struggled to free themselves from Baghdad's rule. Though the opposition groups were able to form themselves into the Joint Action Committee representing 17 different organizations, it seems clear that they were united only in their opposition to Saddam Hussein and that their underlying divisions would mean the end of Iraq and the creation, at least, of a more or less independent Kurdish homeland. The Shias would not accept the secular politics of the Kurds and the Kurds would not agree to anything resembling the fundamentalist theocracy of Iran.

The insurrections throughout Iraq initially made significant inroads into Saddam Hussein's power. In the early stages, the government very nearly lost control of Basra. By the end of the first week of the ceasefire, opposition forces claimed, probably correctly, to be in

control of a number of towns, all of them in the Tigris/Euphrates valley between Baghdad and Basra.

Meanwhile, the Iraqi army was being reorganized and made operational. This was the kind of warfare it was designed for and to which it is best suited. Small wonder that the Joint Action Committee appealed to the Allies for support, even if it was merely to continue to pursue the isolation of Saddam so it "is impressed on the upper echelons of the Iraqi army that nobody will deal with Saddam...They will join in the uprising." But they were to be disappointed. As the insurrection gathered force - in the third week of March most Kurdish territory had been liberated, including the important oil city of Kirkuk - so, too, did the Iraqi army, which was now able to bring in the troops of the Republican Guard, supported in the air by helicopters and aircraft. By the following week, all the urban centres were back under

government control with the loss of much life among civilians suspected of supporting the insurrection. The Shias returned to their homes and Kurdish guerrillas once again took refuge in the mountains. By the beginning of April, many thousands of civilian Kurds were attempting to flee into Turkey or Iran. Saddam Hussein has survived, despite defeat in the Gulf War, despite a for once united opposition, despite Iran's clear call that he should resign.

This "miracle" was in part the consequence of Saddam's hold over important units of the Iraqi army - a community of interests - and his willingness to use it against other Iraqis in a most brutal and lethal way. At the same time, it is clear that the victor states,

---

In the south, encouraged by the US occupation, Shi'ite Muslims rebelled against Saddam. In the end, they too succumbed.

particularly the United States, had no wish to see Iraq collapse. It would raise even more difficult problems for the region if the south cleaved to Iran and the Kurds began a ferment in Turkey and Iran for independence. America's first priority, therefore, was to preserve Iraq's territorial integrity, and then to prevent any strengthening of Iran's position in the Gulf. The fall of Saddam Hussein was desirable but not essential. The only area in which American policy agreed with that of the Joint Action Committee was in the wish for a military coup which would overthrow Saddam, preserve Iraq, but still give scope for political and ethnic improvement.

The Palestinian question
This brings us to some of the more intangible aspects of the ceasefire. It seems likely that US policy, quite apart from specific interests in Iraq and the Gulf, is determined to preserve its

position in the Middle East generally. One of the ironies is that the war has done what Saddam Hussein said he wanted, ie, linked the Gulf crisis with the Palestinian problem. As an Arab peacekeeping force for the Gulf emerges, underpinned by American naval and air power, and as the United States and the Soviet Union continue to cooperate in formulating a common policy in the region, it begins to look as though an easing of positions on all sides might produce progress on Palestine.

Though the US position was enhanced by the war and it found itself for the first time in a position to effect compromises on both sides, it would be a mistake to regard the Soviet Union as without influence in this region. Apart from its long-established connections, Soviet diplomacy throughout the crisis has been balanced and intelligent; it, too, is in a position to effect compromise. The Soviet Union is a major supplier of arms to the Middle East, and so no attempt to reduce the military power of, for instance, Iraq, can succeed without Soviet cooperation.

President Bush's address to Congress in the first week of March focused on a Middle East peace settlement based on a "twin track" approach in which Israeli fears of being overwhelmed in peace conference negotiations would be allayed by simultaneous bilateral talks with neighbouring states, on the one hand, and with the Palestinians, though not necessarily Arafat, on the other. Israel, for its part, had to be prepared to trade "territory for peace".

The formula appears to have created some movement during Secretary of State Baker's tour of the Middle East and Soviet Union. The Israeli Government has invited Saudi Arabia, Syria and Jordan to engage in peace talks and is prepared "to call it a regional conference". Elected Palestinians, though not the PLO, might take part. The eight Arab states of the

"I was suckered..."

GENERAL NORMAN SCHWARZKOPF
(ON SADDAM HUSSEIN)

Home at last. The first US troops to be withdrawn came into Langley AB in Virginia to a rapturous welcome.

coalition, too, have cautiously allowed a "convergence of views", though they continue to press for an international Middle East peace conference. Baker has spoken of his optimism and at the same time has insisted that both sides - he means the Israelis - must be prepared to shift.

The war has added significant dimensions to this process. First, participation across the political spectrum - Syria's attachment to the coalition was critical - has been a balm to Arab pride, wounded in three wars with Israel. Second, Israel, though uneasy, allowed itself to be wrapped in the political and military security blanket of the coalition:

it, too, gained confidence. Third, the Palestinians of the diaspora have a new bitterness to swallow, this time at the hands of their Arab "brothers" in Kuwait. It makes their need for a homeland all the greater and, with the mass exodus from Kuwait, perhaps a more fruitful commitment from the world community to Palestine itself will be found.

It may be that out of the destruction and death will come some kind of Middle East settlement. If so, the Arab-Israeli conflict can only be the beginning, for ultimately any settlement must confront problems of poverty, environmental pollution and damage, and the vexed questions of political difference and religious intolerance. But these problems are not unique to the Middle East. It is here that the world is looking hopefully towards the United Nations, so prominent in the period before the fighting began.

In retrospect, the military operations were a clear success, even if they were curtailed before the subterranean political aims of the coalition were achieved. What might have been foreseen was the immense human tragedy which awaited the Kurds and others.

Nearly two million Kurds fled to Turkey and Iran after the defeat of their uprising. The British Prime Minister's suggestion of "safe havens" for the refugees in northern Iraq, was, after some hesitation, accepted by the US. But it proved difficult to convince the Kurds that the havens - camps such as those created at Cukurca and Zakho - will indeed be safe in the long run. They know, better than most observers of Saddam's regime, that he can be trusted to observe any "autonomy deal" with the Kurds for exactly as long as it can be enforced by a military or police presence.

The long road home - to these refugees that may be Saudi Arabia, Iran, Kuwait, or wherever will take them.

MARKS OF DISTINCTION

Ever since man first made war on man, there has been a need to identify who was friend and who was foe, and so a system of badges or emblems was created. In medieval times these marks became ever more intricate and developed into a science - heraldry.

Even today, this system has survived and is carefully nurtured. A sense of pride in the Regiment, Squadron or Ship is still embodied in the emblem or crest. Some of the most colourful examples can be found in the US and Canadian armed forces and the badges shown below are randomly selected from the many that were emblazoned on vests, arms and chests of the servicemen from those countries.

Full colour examples have been chosen rather than the drabber, two-tone examples often seen on combat dress today.

TACTICAL AIR COMMAND

US AIR FORCES IN EUROPE

MILITARY AIRLIFT COMMAND

914 TACTICAL AIRLIFT GROUP [AIR FORCE RESERVE]

911 TACTICAL AIRLIFT GROUP [AIR FORCE RESERVE]

907 TACTICAL AIRLIFT GROUP [AIR FORCE RESERVE]

10 TACTICAL FIGHTER WING [USAFE]

494 TFS, 48 TACTICAL FIGHTER WING [USAFE]

101 AIRBORNE DIVISION (AIR ASSAULT) [US ARMY]

409 SQUADRON CANADIAN AIR FORCE

CREDITS

Picture Credits:
Associated Press; Steve Bent/Katz Pictures; Steve Bent/Katz Pictures; Associated Press; Rudi Frey/Time Synd/Katz Pictures; Tom Stoddart/Katz Pictures; Barry Iveson/Time Synd/Katz Pictures; Catherine Herog/Time Synd/Katz Pitctures; Tom Stoddart /Katz Pictures (both); Dick Halstead/Time Synd/Katz Pictures; Steve Bent/Katz Pictures; Dennis Brack/Time Synd/Katz Pictures; Patrick Allen (all); Patrick Allen (all); Tom Stoddart/ Katz Pictures (both); Steve Bent/Katz Pictures; Tony O Brien/JB Pictures/Katz Pictures; Alex Quesada/Matrix/Katz Pictures; Associated Press; Associated Press; Charles Sneider/JB Pictures/Katz; Tom Stoddart/Katz Pictures; Tom Stoddart/Katz Pictures (both); Charles Steiner/JB Pictures/Katz Pictures; Barry Iveson/Time Synd/Katz Pictures Associated Press; Mark Peterson/JB Pictures/Katz Picures; Associated Press; Associated Press (both); Barry Iveson/Time Synd/Katz Pictures TRH/Katz Pictures, Tom Stoddart/Katz Pictures; Associated Press (both); Ben Gibson/Katz Picures; Nigel Bradley; Charles Steiner/JB Pictures/Katz Pictures; Patrick Allen; A Cambell/Photo Press; Air International (all); Associated Press; Tom Stoddart/Katz Pictures; TRH/Katz Pictures (both); Steve Bent/ Katz Pictures; John Nordell/JB Pictures/Katz Pictures; Roger Hutchings/Katz Pictures (both); Dennis Brack/Time Synd/Katz Pictures, Tom Stoddart/Katz Pictures; Mark Peterson/JB Pictures/Katz Pictures; Associated Press; Tom Stoddart/Katz Pictures; Associated Press; Patrick Allen; A Cambell/Photo Press; Tony O Brien/JB Pictures/Katz Pictures (both); Mark Peterson/JB Pictures/Katz Pictures; Associated Press; Tom Stoddart/Katz Pictures; Nigel Bradley, Associated Press; John Nordell/JB Pictures/Katz Pictures; Steve Bent/Katz Pictures; TRH/Katz Pictures; Associated Press; Associated Press; Associated Press; Steve Bent/Katz Pictures (both); Steve Bent/Katz Pictures; Dennis Brack/Time Synd/Katz Pictures; Associated Press; Steve Bent/Katz Pictures; Associated Press (both); Lyndsay Peacock; Tom Stoddart/Katz Pictures McDonnell Douglas; Tom Stoddart/Katz Pictures; Thomas Hartwell/Time Synd/Katz Pictures; Tom Stoddart/Katz Pictures; Steve Bent/Katz Pictures; Steve Bent/Katz Picures; Associated Press; Steve Bent/Katz Pictures (left), David Reynolds/Photo Press; David Reynolds/Photo Press; Ben Gibson/Katz Pictures; Steve Bent/Katz Pictures; Steve Bent/Katz Pictures; David Leeson/Dallas Morning News/JB Pictures/Katz Pictures; David Leeson/Dallas Morning News/JB Pictures/Katz Pictures; Rina Castelnuovo/Time Synd/Katz Pictures; Roger Hutchings/Katz Pictures; Tom Stoddart/Katz Pictures; John Reardon/Katz Pictures; William Cambell/Time Synd/Katz Pictures; John Reardon/Katz Pictures; Nigel Bradley (all); Associated Press.

Editorial and design direction: *Nigel Bradley*
Editor: *Alexa Stace*
Production: *Susan Brown*

Maps and diagrams: *Line and Line*
Full colour artworks: *Ken Aitken*
Aircraft profiles: *Air International*

For help and advice in compiling this book the publisher would like to thank: Susan Glen of Katz Pictures, Nancy Holloway of the BBC World Service, David Reynolds, John Stace and Barry Wheeler of *Air International*.